Victor's Story

a father teaches his daughter life's most important lessons

MARYANNE SHAW

Victor's Story
a father teaches his daughter life's most important lessons
By: Maryanne Shaw

© 2015 Maryanne Shaw, All Rights Reserved

Cover design by: Jrabelo Dreamstime.com - Boy Fishing With Dog in River photo

"This book is designed to provide information in regard to the subject matter covered. It is written with the understanding that the publisher is not engaged in rendering medical, religious or psychological advice and does not intend this as a substitute for care by qualified professionals.

All rights reserved. Printed in the United States of America. No part of this booklet may be reproduced in any form or by any electronic or mechanical means including information storage and retrieval systems without permission in writing from the publisher, except by a reviewer who may quote brief passages in a review.

Published by: Shaw Creative
PO Box 703
Uniontown, OH 44685

ISBN: 978-0-9906362-2-9 Paperback
ISBN: 978-0-9906362-3-6 eBook

Library of Congress Cataloging-in Publication Data

Printed in the United States of America

2nd Edition
Printing 12 11 10 9 8 7 6 5 4 3 2

Dedication:
For you Dad, I finally got it done!

By Maryanne Shaw:

Victor's Story
a father teaches his daughter life's most important lessons
The 9 Week Miracle
http://www.maryanneshaw.com

The Marcy D. Nicholas Books:

Angel Stories from Across America
Amish Gardening Secrets
The Household Companion
The Food Remedy Handbook
2009 Ways to Live Simply, Smarter, Healthier & Stress Free
The Gardening Book: Tricks, Tips & Secrets of the Trade
Herbs: Nature's Pharmacy or Nature's Poison?
Guide to America's Best Getaways
Natural Home Remedies for Pets

The former Remedy of the Day Daiy Internet Column as well as these informative booklets:

72 Secrets to Look Younger
Headaches: Is There a Quick Fix?
How to Grow, Dry, Use & Prepare Herbs
Anti-Aging Tips
Use It or Lose It: Home Remedies for your Mind!
Training & Traveling Tips for your Pet
Garlic: Nature's Antibiotic
199 Things Your Mother Used to Tell You
Beware of Identity Theft

Table of Contents

Dedication
Preface
Introduction

Chapter 1:
    It all Began in Waynesburg, Ohio 9

Chapter 2:
    Boyhood Days 13

Chapter 3:
    School Days 33

Chapter 4:
    Life in Waynesburg, Ohio 53

Chapter 5:
    Working Days 93

Chapter 6:
    Courtship 103

Chapter 7:
    Family 109

Chapter 8:
    Down Memory Lane 119

Chapter 9:
    Life Lessons Through a Daughter's Eyes 123

Chapter 10:
    To Josephine 145

Chapter 11:
    Recipes 151

Chapter 12:
    Pictures 157

    About the Author 166

Preface

This book was a long time in the making. Over thirty years to be exact. It all started back in January 1983 when my dad had the idea to record the adventures of his boyhood days onto a cassette tape. As his stories filled tape after tape, he realized he had quite a bit to tell! When he turned off the tape recorder for the last time, he made a copy of the set of tapes for each of his five children.

I remember listening to the tapes for the first time, laughing and shaking my head at his antics. Parts of the tapes drove me to tears. He was quite a man, my dad. In fact, he was my mentor.

There are so many life lessons he taught me, lessons about faith, integrity, kindness, generosity, love, bravery and gratitude. I remember telling dad that I wanted to write a book about his life and adventures. This got him all excited. He got to asking me, "Are you done yet? How much have you got? You'd better hurry up, or I won't be around to see it!"

Years past and I never did get that project complete. Then he got sick. I worked on it in earnest. I got about 60% complete with the book before he died. After that I couldn't bear to turn the tape recorder on and hear the sound of his voice. The recorder stayed silent for many years. Until now.

When I turned the tape recorder on after all these years and my dad's voice boomed through the speakers, it was like he was here in the room with me. I had been a little anxious to hear his voice again, but my fears were put immediately to rest. It was wonderful to hear him again! All the years melted away, and I was able to complete this project, this labor of love, quite effortlessly. As I said, it was like he was standing right here beside me. And you know what? He probably was…

Authors Note: This book has been transcribed directly from the tapes that are in my dad's own words. They contain no corrections for grammar. To read it is like listening to him talk. It is his voice.

Throughout the various stories, he stops and starts the tape recorder. As he turns the machine off and on, each time he said something like, *"I'll come back later on," "Bye for now," "Good morning. It's me again,"* and my favorite, *"Until we meet again"*. When he got close to the end of each side of the tape, he would play what he called his *"Theme song."* It was a lively tune that he called *"My Treasure"* but I wasn't able to really identify it. The song was played over and over again to finish up each side of the tape. He enjoyed making these tapes as much as we cherish having them.

Introduction

This is Victor DiCola.

I went to the doctor on the 22nd of January 1983 and found out I have pneumonia. So I've been in the house recording these tapes. I thought I'd spend my time recording some stories of my boyhood days, and I started making these tapes.

On the year 19 and 6, I was born. The date was September the 23rd. I was born in a little town called East Palestine, Ohio, Columbiana County. We lived by a brick yard. My dad worked in a brick yard, and I was born in the company's brick homes that they had close to the brick yard. I don't remember much of that town because we soon moved away from there.

My brother, Herman, was born in 1905, the year before me. We moved to Canton, Ohio on Madison Avenue which is now occupied by the Diebold Lock & Safe Company. So my dad worked at the Royal Brick yard at the time and again I don't remember much of Canton. The only thing I know is that my brother, Pat was born there. From Canton, we moved to Magnolia. Again we lived in company houses close to the brick yard. This time he worked for the Whitacre Greer Fireproofing Company. And we lived in company houses again.

In those days we were poor, you know, no electric lights, just a little cook stove in the house. My sister, Mary was born in Magnolia. I don't remember much about that town, I was just a little infant at the time too, but then we moved to Waynesburg where my dad worked at the brick yard. And that's the town that I grew up in.

Chapter 1.

It all Began in Waynesburg, Ohio

To be happy, fathers must always be giving; it is ceaselessly giving that makes you really a father.
        Goriot, in *PERE GORIOT* by Honore de Balzac [1]

In the very southern part of Stark County Ohio is a little town called Waynesburg along the banks of the Big Sandy creek. The first cabin built there was in 1815 by Captain James Downing. The area was overrun with snakes, thick trees and rocky hills. Early pioneers and Indians had passed through this territory for many years prior to Captain Downing's first arrival to the area back in 1793. In 1816 the town began to grow slowly. The Village of Waynesburg was incorporated in February 1833. [2]

Waynesburg now has a little fewer than 1000 residents. When my father's parents moved there in 1910, the community of Waynesburg was quite small. But let's back up a bit.

My grandfather, Giacomo DiCola was born May 11, 1874 in Roccaraso, Italy to Ascanio DiCola and the former Giovanna Dal Dorio. A second child, a boy named Pasqulino was born but only lived to the age of 8. Young Giacomo tended the flocks as a shepherd along with his father up until the age of 22. In the year 1896 Giacomo set sail for America hoping to secure a good life. For almost 8 years he toiled digging ditches sending a portion of his earning to help support his parents. He returned home to Italy to warmly embrace his father as his mother had passed away. Upon his return he courted and married Elizabetta Trilli.

My grandmother was born September 5, 1882 also in Roccaraso Italy and christened Elizabetta, or Sabita. After my grandparents were married for almost one year and had welcomed the birth of their first child, Giovanna on May 1, 1904 they departed Italy for America.

---

   1   Goriot, in PERE GORIOT by Honore de Blazac
   2   History of Wynesburg, Sesqui-Centennial 1833-1983, Clyde Mann

Arriving in New York in the winter of 1904 the small family settled in East Palestine, Ohio. Sadly on February 14, 1905 the baby died after getting sick during the passage. See pages 24-25. A son, Armando (Herman) was welcomed in 1905 and then on September 23, 1906 Vittorio (Victor) was born. My father.

The family left East Palestine in 1907 due to scarcity of work and settled in Canton, Ohio. Another son was born there, Pasqualino (Patsy or Pat). Still struggling, my grandfather got a job in the brickyard in Magnolia, Ohio and moved the family there. In 1910 a little girl named Mary was welcomed to the family.

Soon a chance to earn better wages that included a rent-free home owned by the brickyard caused the family to move to Waynesburg. In 1911 another boy was born, little Baradeno (Ben). In 1913 another son arrived, Orlando. But this baby only lived 7 months. (See page 113-114 for the story) 1914 brought the birth of another son, Lorenzo (Lawrence) and 1916 another boy Giovanni (John). The family was rounded out in 1919 with the birth of a little girl, Giovanna (Jenny) to commemorate not only my great grandmother, but the child that was lost so soon after arriving in America.

My grandfather worked in the coal mine and my grandmother tended their store, baked bread and looked after the large family. My grandfather was drafted into service for World War I but the war ended before he had to actually go.

The DiCola family left Waynesburg on August 18, 1922 and headed back to Canton, Ohio for the first time since 1907.

The stories included in this book are in my father's words and detail his early days in Waynesburg and that of their family life so I won't attempt to summarize them here. I think it's important to note that the booklet, *The History of Waynesburg* mentions the Civil War US army surgeon, Dr. G. A. Shane along with Dr. E. G. McCormick. Both of these doctors are featured in my dad's stories. Also of note is that the author of the booklet, Clyde Mann grew up to be a journalist. His name also appears within the stories.

A second anthology called *A History of Sandy Valley* includes the Village of Waynesburg. This was written by F. C. Orlando Sr. This is none other than little Frankie featured in the story on pages 88-89.

Also mentioned frequently throughout the narrative is the big barn. Orlando's compilation says this:

> *It was the largest structure of the kind in town, and was as well finished as any other whereabouts, but in this whole construction, there was not a single piece of sawed lumber used. Doors, door frames, floors, shingles, everything in the shape of lumber was made by splitting it from trees cut nearby, and every nail used and there were not many, was made by the village blacksmith.* [3]

One of my favorite tales is the one about the homemade sled that appears on page 13-14. In Orlando's account he tells about The Old Red Jumper:

> *The tale of the red jumper goes back to the early winter of 1909 when the village, then a prosperous brick manufacturing town, decided to have a large bob sled built to furnish a winter sport for the older men of the community. A collection was taken, the material purchased and the sled was constructed. The jumper when finished was 12 feet long and 18 inches wide with a large foot guider. The course was selected as old State Route No. 30, now South Main Street and became known as the mile a minute sleighing course of Stark County. The jumper after getting under way at full speed would strike a hump in the road and would jump 15 to 20 feet. Only one serious accident occurred and if it hadn't been for high wheels on freight cars at the time, several lives might have been lost. But as it was, the boys who came screaming down the hill just as a freight train pulled into the station, slid off the sled and others stretched as flat as they could. Several were knocked unconscious when the jumper passed under a boxcar while the rest went merrily on their way down the road around the sharp curves to the old mill.* [3]

My dad was one of those who went merrily on their way down the road!

---

3   A History of Sandy Valley, F.C. Orlando Sr

Chapter 2.

Boyhood Days

There are three ways to get something done:
 1. *Do it yourself.*
 2. *Hire someone to do it for you.*
 3. *Forbid your kids to do it.*

Author Unknown [4]

Now growing up in Waynesburg was a lot of fun. It was the best time of my life. In that town I was a real "Huckleberry Finn." In the summer we used to hike through the woods with the dogs. We'd pick berries and mushrooms, look for chestnuts and things like that. We loved to go to the barn and play in the straw.

Of course we always went swimming too. We spent all of our time outside and made our way home just as hungry as a bear. In the winter there was skating and sleigh riding.

Winter time:

I remember as a kid that the snow on the ground lasted all winter round. And we made our own sleds, you know, our parents couldn't afford to buy us sleds. We used to go down those Waynesburg hills.

I remember one time when we went through downtown. We had a big bobsled. Big, red and we used to keep it in the little fire station. It was a sled with a 2-wheel cart with a hose. Back then that was considered a fire truck. The men would have to pull it to put out fires. That is what they used. The bobsled was kept in there. So ten or twelve of us kids from the hill, we called it the hill, that's where the company houses were. We took this bobsled up the big long hill. Oh it was about 2 miles long going way up this hill.

So we went up this hill, and when we reached the top we'd get on this here bobsled, and down the hill we would go. Oh boy, I wanna tell

---

 4 Author Unknown

you, it was fun. And we'd go through the public square there, you know. And of course they had no traffic lights at that time, and the horse and buggy's seen us coming. We whizzed through the public square, and down that hill. And down below was a railroad track. And wouldn't you know a freight train was passing and we couldn't get stopped. That freight train was stopped right across the railroad crossing with a box car that had enough clearance under it for the bobsled to pass, but we couldn't get through it because our heads would be knocked off if we did.

So we all shouted, "Put your heads down!" and "Lean backwards as far as you can!" We were gonna try to go under the box car. So we all leaned backwards each putting their head on the chest of the boy behind him. We whizzed under the train and we made it! Down the next hill and down to the Big Sandy creek where it came to stop right in the river. The front part sank in getting the driver of the sled wet. We climbed out, and we were happy that we made it. Up the hill we headed to go again for another run. But when we got to the square everybody had seen what we had done. They took the sled away from us and said, "You kids go on home. Don't you ever get this bobsled again." Of course our parents found out, and then there was heck to pay.

In the winter we'd sit around the big pot belly stove. My dad had bought one of those round pot belly stoves with a grill around it. We would gather around there and everybody would tell stories and stuff. My dad would always tell the story about what happened to me when I lived in Waynesburg which I didn't remember at the time because I was just small.

This story has been repeated over and over. Back in those days we had outhouses. When they got full, they would dig a new hole and move it back further. Then they would cover up the hole that was full with ashes. This particular time the man from the brick yard never delivered the ashes. So the next morning me and the neighbor boy were walking down from the field. We walked, and wouldn't you know that we walked right into it and sunk into this outhouse right up to our chins!

Oh, we screamed and hollered and our hands were smashing, you know, trying to grab. Oh you can imagine, the outhouse stuff was all over us. And eeew we were a mess and smelled! The women started screaming and hollering "You know that Victor and this other boy fell in the outhouse!"

Men came running and pulled us out. Oh we were a mess, just like a tar baby from head to foot. And stink! So the women took two big wash tubs, and my mother put me in this wash tub. They had to practically cut the clothes off me because they were so filthy. Heh heh. They put me in that water and they scrubbed me with everybody around. That was really something.

One particular winter it was icy, and we decided to go see a steam shovel. In those days the shovels didn't have any motors, just steam belching smoke, digging for shale on the side of the hill. We decided we wanted to see that shovel. We climbed a hill and made it down all right. Pat took a wrong turn and slid headlong down that cliff and hit his face against a big boulder. He cut his lip clear through to his tongue and he was bleeding. Some of the other boys were saying "Pat fell! Pat fell!"

I didn't hear them at first because the shovel was making so much noise steaming and hissing. I went back and picked him up and carried him. I remember I took a rock and punched a hole through the ice and got water and washed his face. That was the worst thing I could have done because that water made his jaw swell up the size of a baseball. We took him home and my handkerchief was covered with blood, you know. He hid behind the pot belly stove we had. We told mom "Pat got hurt." And mom said "Good for you, I told you kids not to go out in this kind of weather and you kids don't listen to nothing!" And she wasn't moving. We raised our voices ,"He has blood on his face." She got up, "Let me see." She took one look and cried "Oh filla mia, what did you do?" She called the doctor. It took four or five stitches to sew up the wound.

It was one of those winter days, and oh it was cold. Snow was deep outside and the wind was blowing that snow around. When you looked out the window and saw one of the neighbors pass by, the wind was a blowin' his coat. He was walking hunched back holdin' his hat and that wind was just whirlin'. It was no time to be out, you know. That's why we were in the house. Nothin' to do and I was getting' kind of restless. I always used to pick on my sister, Mary. She was right there in the kitchen. Mom was in the back room doing work, preparing supper; she always had something to do.

My sister would pass by me and I'd grab her hair. She had a big, long pigtail made in braids. And I used to catch that pigtail and pull it "Ma! Vic's pulling my hair!" "Vittorio, if you don't keep your arms to yourself I'll break 'em!" Of course she would never break 'em, you know, but I would stop for a while. Mary would just look at me satisfied that Mom scolded me. She would walk up and down, and I'd call her Gypsy. "Get out of here Gypsy." And she resented that. "Ma! He's calling me Gypsy!" "Gypsy! Gypsy!" She gave me a little push, and I got a hold of her hair and gave it three big yanks. "Ma! Ma! He's pulling my hair again! Mom!" "Vittorio! If I come in there I'll give you a cuff in the face!" Well, I kept quiet for a while.

And Mary kept going up and down in the kitchen passing in front of me. And I wasn't touching her. The next time she came by, I grabbed a hold of her pigtail and I gave it a yank and pulled it way down. It brought her head down, her chin was up in the air, and I held her there "Ma! Maaaa! He's pulling my hair!" Oh my mother got mad. She came in there. "How many times do I tell you to leave her alone?" I knew mom was mad, so I knew it was time to quit.

I went to the window. It was all frozen over. I scraped a hole and scraped some of the ice off the window and made a big round hole and put my lips to it, you know and blew on it to get the heat to melt the ice. I looked out. There the wind was blowing, twisting around. It was a cold and windy day, deep snow. So I said "Ma, I have to go pee." Now the outhouses are in the back of the yard, a little distance away. She said "Well put on your coat and your hat and go." I put on my coat and my hat and opened that door. Oh, that wind, was a blowin' and the snow drift was so high. Up to my knees it was as I made my way to the outhouses, pluggin' through that deep snow and drifts. I got to the outhouses and did my business there. Naturally I peed all over the seat and got the seat wet. By the time I got my coat buttoned up, that pee all over that toilet seat had frozen to ice. Oh, it was cold.

I huddled up, you know, I hurried. I come back in the house near that wood stove, Brrrrrr! I warmed my hands, boy it was cold. That's some of the things I did on some of those bad days when we couldn't get out to play.

During the First World War, there was an epidemic all over the country. It was the Spanish Flu, and they called it influenza. And everybody was catching the flu. It was very dangerous. People were dying all over the country, it was terrible.

Half of the children on the hill were sick and even the parents were sick. One of the boys named Cesar died of the flu. Several older men died from the flu too. Back then, they used to quarantine the house. Once you got the flu they put a big, red sign that said "Quarantine." Some of the parents used to slip out of the windows to go help out the neighbors. You weren't allowed to do it. But a lot of families were in bad shape with nobody to take care of them. Our parents used to slip in and out of the windows too.

Our house was hit with it. My dad and my mother, they had the flu. And she used to get up in the morning and just drag herself to take care of the children. My sisters and most of my brothers got it. Pat and I were the only ones who never got it. I don't know why, but we didn't.

I remember we had this homemade sled with a box nailed onto it. We would walk to the farm to buy old chickens. Mom said, "Go to the farm and get some chickens." She made a lot of chicken soup. That was good for the flu. I remember Pat and I, we'd take that sled. Oh, the snow was up to our knees and we'd tug through that snow. We had a thing called felt boots. There was a rubber boot on the bottom, and the felt went inside the boot with heavy stockings in there. It kept our feet nice and warm. Pat and I had a pair of those. They were called felt boots. And a shawl was around our neck with our ears covered up. Our nose used to get red.

We'd go down the brickyard hill, across the bridge over the Big Sandy River, up to the farm. We would buy 2 or 3 old chickens. Pat gave the farmer the money. We'd put 'em in a box with a lid on top so the chickens wouldn't get away. Of course we had their legs tied. We would come home, and mom in all her misery and weakness used to come there and tell us what to do. "Now boil the water, now pull the feathers out." And she would cut it up, but she would struggle. She would make everyone a big bowl of soup.

I remember when we all had to be vaccinated. Our old country doctor, Dr. McCormick, in his horse and buggy came up the hill. That was the law, we all had to be vaccinated against this here influenza. So Dr. McCormick sat us down in a chair and he would take a needle. He would scratch on your arm and oh, they would make 'em big in those days, as big as a half a dollar. Then they used to put a cup on it, made of plastic. That was the worst thing. We found out later on it was better to keep it open, let the air hit it and it would heal faster. Boy that thing would swell up and fill that cup full with pus. Finally we'd pull it out and wash it off and it would heal and make a big scab. Up to this day I have a big mark on my arm as big as a quarter. I'll show it to you if you want to see it. It's still there.

And that's what we did, and we survived the flu. Hundreds and hundreds of people died, thousands throughout the country. That was the worst epidemic that there was. The flu that we have today, they have medications for it, they can do something for it. But back in my day, it was something new. They didn't know anything about it. In the First World War all the poisonous gas and all the dead soldier's corpses and decay caused that epidemic and that's what that flu was.

We always had good, cold long winters. All the sills were covered with snow. The rabbits were hoppin' off into the fields into some little bush to find shelter. As a boy we would take off. We'd go trappin', skatin' on the pond or we'd go down to the brickyard. We'd take our homemade sleds. There were a lot of hills there. We'd go all the way to the top of the hill behind the house and slide down right to the end. So then that's the way we'd spend our winters, sleigh riding and snow balling and things like that.

Summer time:

One morning when we got up, it was summer time, you know vacation. There was no school. And me and a friend of mine called Pete, Pete Vinci, and two or three other boys would fool around. Of course we always had a bunch of dogs along. We liked to go down to the brick yard and walk around to see how the men would do their work. We liked to watch how they would load tiles into the box cars. There was one of these big smokestacks, the kilns where they cooked the bricks. They put them into these round kilns and they fired it. That's how they make the bricks hard when they bake them.

I always had a fascination to go up to those big stacks where the smoke comes out. They have these iron pegs like steps inside of the bricks that go all the way up to the top. I said to myself, "I want to go up there and see how that smoke comes out from the top." So I started climbing up, you know, and I got about to the middle and one of those iron steps pulled out of the mortar. "Oh my gosh, what am I gonna do now?"

I couldn't go up or down, and I was afraid that if I would fall I would fall backward, and there was nothing for me to hold. So I kinda figured out, I'd give the iron a twist. By giving it a twist, it would kind of bind it in there and it would hold. It worked and I made it! As I passed on top, my foot hit that peg and it fell off, cling clang, down to the bottom it went leaving a big gap there. But I kept going and climbed on top.

When I got to the top, I tried to peep in. Oh, I got a mouthful of that smoke! My eyes burned and that sulphur smell was in my nose. I coughed and I backed down pretty quick when I got that hot smoke into my face. I couldn't see in there like I thought I could. So I start coming down. Now here I come to the place where the step was gone. "Oh my God, how am I gonna get down there?" I was too small and my legs couldn't reach the next step. So I figured what I had to do was to stretch as far as I can, let go of my hand and catch the step below.

I didn't want to do it, I was afraid to do it, but I had to do something. And I done it! And lucky enough I hit the step all right and I caught it, and boy I scrambled down fast. When I got down to the bottom, there was a bunch of men around there. I found out later they were saying "Don't say a word to him. He might get excited and he'll fall. Just let him go, and let him work it out." So when I got down the foreman got me by the shoulders and he turned me and booted me in the pants. He said "You kids get the heck out of this brick yard; you know you could have got killed up there! Why did you go up in those stacks? Those stacks aren't safe enough to go up!" And he drove us out of the brick yard. That's the way I spent some of my summers, doing foolish things as that.

We started our summer vacation in April. In a small town we got out early. In the big city the kids got out of school in June. The first thing we did was go swimming. The weather was nice and warm at the time. In those days you had good warm summers and cold winters. You could always depend on a good summer or a cold winter. And we would walk down the railroad tracks, you know, going down past the brick yard around our famous swimming hole just around the bend. We would go in there and say "Last one in is a monkey!"

All of us back in those days would go bare foot, you know, we wore no shoes. It was April and we could go bare footed. When we got down to the river, all we had to do was just step out of our pants and jump in the water. Of course we couldn't swim. We knew the place wasn't very deep. Up to our chests, and we'd splash water around there and play. Oh, we'd have a diving board there and we would swim. That's how we passed the time.

On another occasion, we were just taking a walk through the woods. On our way back home walking through the brick yard, it was getting kind of late, kind of dusk you know. The sun was just setting in the west, big sky you know. So we were walking home through the brick yard and passed through a big salt shanty. Now I didn't see this, but my brother, Pat, he stopped and whispered "Look!" and right in that salt shanty he said there was a red devil with a pitch fork and a big forked tail. I stared at him as he whispered louder, "There's a devil!" We ran out of there so doggone fast it looked like we had wings. And ohhhh did we run, we were so scared. And we ran and ran until we got out of there. By that time we were about a mile away from the salt shanty. I asked "What did you see?" Pat insisted "The devil, you see it?" I didn't take a look, I just beat it, boy. I didn't take any chances and look at it. I took his word for it and I ran. And of course when we went home we just kept it quiet. We never used to tell our parents all the things we did.

Another time during the summer we took all the dogs together and we decided we'd take a hike through the woods. We went into these here woods along the Big Sandy. It was a nice big river, pretty wide, you know. We used to fish and swim and in those days it was clear. You could see down to the bottom. It wasn't polluted, it was beautiful. We drank out of that river many a times.

Well, going through this field there was a bunch of cows and on the other end there was a bull. Now the dogs were making so much fuss barking at this bull, that the bull would start chasing us. And oh, didn't that bull come at us. There was a fallen tree that was about halfway into the middle of the river. So we went up the trunk of this tree and stayed there until the bull went back to his herd. So we scrambled out and started going across the field again to reach the other side where the woods were. And the bull would see us, and start chasing after us again, and this time there was no tree to run into.

We ran until we came to a barbwire fence. It had about three strands of barbwire, just enough clearance on the bottom to skid under it. And when we went there, we just dove under that there fence, tearing our shirts on barb wire. Some kids got their back scratched, but we all made it across that fence. That bull came, and he hit that wire fence. I wanna tell you that wire fence bent like a slingshot, BOOM! It must have hurt the bull, because he didn't try it again. That's the way we got across that there meadow.

So we walked, and by this time we were thirsty. We came to an old, abandoned farmhouse. Oh, we were thirsty from running, you know, and walking. There was one of those old pumps there, all rusty, that you had to prime it to get the water out. If you know how those old pumps in those days were, you had to lift up the handle, and the water would drop down to the bottom. Then what you had to do is take some water, put it on top and that primes it so you could pump and get your water out. So I thought, "What are we going to do to prime it?" There was no water around, and we left the river pretty far back.

So I came up with an idea. "All right all you boys, all you boys got to pee in this can so we can put it in that pump there. And if you don't pee, you don't drink!" Everybody piped up "I have to pee!" So we peed, and put it in there. We yelled "C'mon pee!" One guy said "No, I can't!" We told him "You better pee, or you ain't gonna drink!" So he forced some, every little bit counts! So we put it in that pump and started pumping, pumping and wouldn't you know here comes the water. We pumped it for a while, you know. We were smart; we left that dirty water out on top to wash out. Boy did we drink! We would cup our hands and get that water. Oh, was that water fresh! That water tasted so good. We wet our head, put our head under it. After we had our fill, I said, "Heck, I ain't gonna leave it like that. Let somebody else do the same thing we had to do." So I pushed the handle up then I let it go and down went the water. You'd have to prime it again if you wanted it. So that's how we got our drink.

We went across on the other side of the road and there was an old swinging bridge there. What it consists of is two cables tied to a tree on each side and a little board in the middle, like a little plank going across the river. Then there were two wires up above which were so high us kids couldn't reach it until you got to the middle when the wires swung down lower, then you could reach it.

Well we got up there you know and started to go across it. My brother, Ben, he was afraid. He was crying, "I'm afraid, I'm afraid!" He wanted to carry the dog across because our dog, Topsy was whining. Ben begged "Let's carry him across." We said "No, let him swim." Ben cried "No, he won't swim!" So Herman went back and picked Topsy up. Ben, he was crying. He thought the dog was gonna drown. Herman took Topsy about half way across the bridge and said "All right, you're gonna learn to swim now or never." So he took him threw him over the bridge right in the middle, right down in the water. Boy didn't that dog swim! He swam toward shore, shook hisself off, hopping around. He wasn't happy. Topsy sure could swim. Now all the other kids went across, even Ben. That's the way we got across this here swinging bridge.

I want to talk about our dog, Topsy. Now my brother, Ben, always considered Topsy his dog. He had his own name for him. He always called Topsy, Pokey. He'd say "Here Pokey, Here Pokey, Here Pokey, Here Pokey." I'd tell Ben "Don't call him Pokey, his name is Topsy!" Ben would always whine, "Aww he's Pokey, I call him Pokey." And the dog learned to respond. The dog took a liking to Ben. He always would feed the dog, and he would hug and squeeze the dog, and he would hold the dog and play with him more than us boys did, and he would give it food from time to time so naturally he would take on to Ben. He would say "C'mon Pokey, C'mon Pokey", and the dog would follow him. Ben insisted on calling him Pokey, but I always called him Topsy.

So it was another nice day in the summer, and all of us boys decided to play some kind of a game, we were always playing some kind of a game. There was a little boy up on the hill name of Bruno. He was a sick little boy. We didn't know it at the time, we always thought he was a sissy. We would pick sides, and he would always come on my side. We used to just run up and down there right in the middle of a dirt road. Very few cars would pass by and when one would come by we naturally would move aside to leave it by. It was an old car going by, usually a model-T Ford. Then we'd get back on the road. And little Bruno he wanted to play. So I said, "Let him play."

So Bruno came in there and started playing. We were all running you know and we were kinda rough. Bruno got pushed by somebody and he fell and kind of bruised his knee a little bit. Boy he started sobbin' and cryin'. Ohh poor kid he was sobbin' and cryin'. His mother heard and said "Bambino! What did you do to my little Bambino! What did you do to my little child?" He had a sister named Bruna. See his name was Bruno and her name was Bruna. Almost sounds the same. So Bruna came up to get her brother. She yelled at us "What did you do to my little brother?" We told her, "We didn't do nothing! He just fell." Bruno cried, "Waaaa He pushed me! That kid pushed me!" His sister Bruna just grabbed her brother with a "C'mon Bruno."

She took him home. The kid was sobbin' and cryin'. About an hour later he appeared by his door, watchin' us. He was a pitiful little sight. His mother would never allow him to play with us again, he never was allowed to come down the hill to play with us because she thought we were a little bit too rough for him and he might get hurt. He was kind of sickly like, and I felt sorry for him. The boy was always sick and he wasn't going to school much.

One day the teacher asked "Why isn't Bruno at school, he hasn't been at school for a long time, why isn't he at school?" One boy answered, "They said he's sick but I don't believe he's sick because I always see him outside playing, he's always playing outside. He's not too sick to play outside, but he's too sick to come to school." The teacher said "Does anybody know for sure if you see him play?" Another boy said "Yes, I see him play." So I got mad and said, "Now listen, now wait a minute now. Sure the boy is playing. The poor boy is sick, he has construction." In those days we called tuberculosis construction, today they call it TB. So I insisted, "The boy is sick. The doctor said he needs exercise and fresh air and that's why he is outside playing." The teacher said "I'm sorry to hear that, I didn't know the boy was sick." So she left it go at that.

Well as each day went on, the boy was getting worse and worse. He wasn't getting any better, and we didn't see him out playing. He was more confined to his house. We hadn't seen him, but didn't think much of it. One morning we heard little Bruno died. Oh, we were so sorry for him. We kind of took a liking to him after we knew he was really sick. We were so sorry for the poor boy. And they had him in the home there. In those days they didn't take them to the funeral parlor, they just showed them in the homes.

His mother said to us in Italian, "Do you want to come in and see my little Bambino? All you boys who used to play with my little Bambino?" We said, "Yea, we'd like to see your Bruno." So all us boys, I remember going into this Bruno's house, and there he lay in a coffin. He had a nice blue suit on, a white shirt, and he looked pale, and he looked real white, and he just lay there. And we were just so sorry for him. Ohhh.

Talking about babies dying, I remember the time when my little baby (brother) Orlando got sick. He died. Now we didn't know anything about death, and that the baby died. I remember my little baby lying in the little white coffin, with two chairs in front right by the window. He had just died, and mom was crying. I asked "The baby has been sleeping a long time, when is he gonna wake up?" And mom was crying and didn't know how to tell us that the baby went with God. God had taken him to heaven.

I remember the undertaker came. I'll never forget he came and he took the little baby. In those days we used to put a long nice white dress on the baby folded under up under his feet, you know. He layed him in this white coffin right by the window by the two chairs and put a nice white blanket on top of the baby His eyes were still open.

I remember him taking a stick, like a match, and taking cotton. He put cotton under one eye and did the same to the other eye. Then he put his hand over his face and the baby's eyes would be closed. It would look like the baby was asleep. We'd say "Ma the baby's asleep. Yea, the baby's asleep, yea." And she cried, you know. And we reached over and touched the little baby's hand. His hand wasn't folded or crossed. They were long, so soft and nice.

Then the following day the undertaker came with a horse and buggy and took the little coffin. He closed the lid. I remember my mother went into the bedroom, and oh how my mother cried. Oh, how mom cried. I remember her crying, you know. And he took the little coffin under his arm and put it into his buggy. Oh, how it was raining that day, oh it was raining. My dad had a long black raincoat on. They put these little crosses at the foot of the buggy. They couldn't put the coffin longways because the buggy was too short. So they put one end down and one end was sticking out over the end. And they took a big tarp and covered the little coffin with that tarp because it was rainin.' Then they went to Morges. My little baby, Orlando was buried in Morges, and that's what I remember about my little baby, Orlando.

When we lived in Waynesburg, Herman had a growth under his throat and it was getting bigger. He could hardly breathe. So we called Dr. McCormick. There was nothing on the outside, it seemed to be all on the inside of his throat. The doctor didn't understand that. He said "Well I don't know much about that." He told us to call old Dr. Shane, an old Civil War doctor that was retired and lived next to the school. He didn't practice anymore. He looked like Colonel Sanders would look. He had a long mustache, you know, white, and a nice, long beard like a goatee.

Herman was getting worse. Every time we got sick mom always put us in her bed. Mom would give up her bed, you know, and sit and watch us all night. Many a night she lost just to take care of us. She couldn't sleep. So we got this Dr. Shane to come over. So he came over in his horse and buggy, old doctor, you know. He walked up to the second floor where Herman was lying in mom's bed.

He told my mother "Get me a hot basin of water," and he felt his throat and said "Um hmm, I've seen many of this stuff, I know what that is. It's inside." It had to be lanced from the inside of his mouth. It was some kind of a growth. In time it would swell and cut off his air, and it would be bad. So my mother got the water ready, and the doctor sterilized his instruments with the water.

Us kids was watching, and I remember he turned Herman's head to the side and put a towel on his face. Herman wouldn't keep his mouth open. So he put some kind of a clamp over Herman's teeth and that kept his mouth open. He couldn't close his mouth if he wanted to. And he got in there and lanced it. Ohhh, out gushed a lot of matter and pus you know. He got his throat and he massaged it and squeezed. He took a long dob with a stick. He painted his throat and took all that infection out and told my mother "Now put a basin here, and every time he has to spit, let him spit that drainage out." And you know he done that, and Herman got better. My mother spent many a night nursing and watching him.

And then another time my brother, Lawrence, he was just a small kid. He had extra large tonsils and they were infected. And oh, he was sick and pale looking. We finally called Dr. McCormick. He looked him over and he said, "These tonsils have to come out. Every time he gets a little cold he gets sick and they just have to come out." We had no hospital in Waynesburg. So my dad got a neighbor that had an old big Buick Touring car. So my dad took little Lawrence, just a small little kid about 3 or 4 years old, no more than that, and took him to Canton to be operated on. My mom sat at home worrying and crying.

When dad came back later on that night, he took him in his arms and gave him to my mother. Lawrence was still out from all the ether. They used to use ether in those days, and he still smelled strong of ether. My dad said "I'm bringing him home more dead than alive. Look what they done to my boy." Mom took him upstairs and put little Lawrence right in the bed, and she nursed him, and she took care of him, and nursed him back to health. Oh gee, she had it hard.

And if that wasn't enough, I remember the time I got pneumonia. I must have caught a chill. I went to bed and I remember I lay right across the bed with my clothes on. When mom came up to put me to bed to undress me, I was burning with sweat. Oh, I had a fever. The only thing I can remember is me being in a little crib right by her bed and she put big plasters on my chest and on my back. When I opened my eyes, I wasn't in my room. I said "Ma, I'm sorry I dirtied the bed!" "No, Filla mia, you didn't dirty the bed, it's a mustard plaster I put on you." So she cleaned me up and took those mustard plasters off. She made chicken soup, fed me by spoon, and she nursed me back to health.

Oh, the nights she lost, and she was tired and still had to do all her hard work. Dad had to work to pay for the doctor bills. It was rough on them. Those were the hard days that my mother and dad had to go through.

I have more adventures from my boyhood days. Some aren't adventures, they are really mean tricks that I done. One of the things that I got a lickin' for that wasn't my fault was this. We lived next door to this other family who had a boy my age, about ten. In the back of the house we always kept our coal in kind of a shed, you know, a bin. He had newspapers in there and kindling wood. We had no gas back in those days. This other boy said, "Let's start a little fire to keep warm." It was a chilly day in autumn so I said "Ok." So he started the fire, and a big blaze went up. There was a lot of coal there, see.

The boy's dad came in there and said, "What are you boy's doing in there, you wanna set the house on fire? Who started that fire?" Well the boy, he was afraid you know to say he did it, so he said "Victor did it." Well his father didn't say a word. He went next door where we lived and got my dad. Here comes my father, and he seen that fire. They put it out first. Then he got me by the neck, and he took me out in the back yard. It was kind of a field where we always played, and boy did he give me a whippin'.

He threw me up in the air, and he bounced me down. Then he'd get me by my hand, and he'd take his foot and he would boot me in the pants, not with the point but with the blunt part of the shoe. Each time he'd give me a boot, I would bounce up, you know, and go around in a circle. And when he hit me again, I'd jump again. Then he would stop that and he would throw me up in the air, and down. I was screamin', and all the neighbors were around watchin'. Finally one man said "Hey, stop that, what do you wanna do, you wanna kill your son?"

Of course, you know I was bawlin'. He stopped and let me go. He was mad because he thought I had caused a lot of problems for our neighbors. I ran and hid under my mother's bed. My mother was worried. She thought he broke every bone in my body. Everybody was around there like it was a big show. So my mother came upstairs and heard me sobbin' and moanin' under the bed. And I put on plenty, you know. "Oh my arm! Oh my leg!" I made it bigger than it was. I was scared of my father more than anything else. It hurt, but I didn't have nothing broke, you know. But I let on as if everything was broke. My mother got me, and she touched me. I'd yelp "Oooh!" Every time she touched me, I let out an ouch! And I was sobbin'. She said, "Now why did you do that, why did you do that Vittorio?" She always called me Vittorio. "Why did you do that Vittorio? You know your father never hits, but when he does his hand is heavy." I said, "I didn't do it mom, I didn't do it!" She said, "You didn't?" I told her the whole story. The boy came in there and he said, "Let's start a fire." So he started a fire. When his father came in there, he was afraid, and he told him, "Victor did it." "His father didn't even ask me, he went and got Pop. He came in there and saw that fire, and he got me, and he beat me."

So my mother, she kind of got me in her arms, you know. Well, she went downstairs, and she talked to my dad. I couldn't hear everything that was said, but my dad, he really felt bad. My dad actually cried. He said, "I could have killed my son." So that made him mad. He went next door and he said, "Listen," I forget the man's name, but he said "Listen, I nearly killed my son, for starting that fire and he didn't do it. He tells me that your boy lit that fire and when you came in there he was afraid, so he lied and he blamed it on Vic. You get your son." So, the neighbor man said, "Son come out here." He got him you know and said "I want you to tell me the truth. Don't you dare lie to your dad." He could see he was pretty scared. "Who stared that fire?" "Well, I did dad, I did. I was afraid, so I said Victor did it." The neighbor said, "Alright, I'll take care of you."

Well he didn't do it like my dad did, whip me out in public. He went back in the house and closed the door. And boy you could hear that kid cryin' and hollerin', you know, heh heh. And my dad was a good, kind man, almost never laid a hand on us. But if we did something wrong, he said, "My hand is heavy."

One day, a beautiful warm summer day, we decided to go out and pick some blackberries so mom could make some blackberry jelly. We took our buckets, Pete Vinci, Romie, my brother, Ben and myself. Well we took off toward the schoolhouse up over the hill that goes toward Morges. That's going west of Waynesburg.

So we went up that hill where the old schoolhouse was and around that nice beautiful road. There was no traffic, nothing back in those days. Every once in a while a horse and buggy or a wagon would come by from one of those farms. We would come to a nice, big field with cows grazing out there in the meadow, beautiful countryside. And here we come to a nice, big patch of berries, oh they were beautiful.

We picked all the black ones we could find, most of them were red. Oh this is a good spot, maybe after they get ripe in about a week we'll come back and pick 'em. So we picked all the blackberries we could find in that particular patch, a lot of berries. They all grow on the side of the road, you know. In those days they grew almost anywhere. So we picked all we could get that was black. We went down about half a mile or so and we came across another patch. Ohh we picked nice blackberries, oh they were beautiful. And we kept on moving and we ran into another beautiful patch. Ohh we picked and picked and picked until the bucket was almost half full. Now these were big buckets!

Then some farmer's dogs saw us there and started barking. They took after us and oh, we got scared. Boy we ran. My brother Ben, was slower, "Cmon Ben, run, run, that dog will bite us." So we ran, and we took the first road to the left. Now we wanted to go to the right toward Morges. But since that dog was chasing us we took the first road that we could find. We went down that there country lane. It looked like a little narrow lane, and Pete said "I was never down here before but I suppose there's berries back here too." We didn't want to turn back with that dog back there. So we kept goin', lookin' for more berries.

Aww, we come to another beautiful patch, and we picked all the nice big blackberries. We didn't pick the small ones. So we picked some big ones and kept on movin'.

Aww, by this time we were so dry and thirsty from running and that dog chasin' us, and there was no place to get a drink. Ohh we wished we just had a cold drink of water. We kept walkin' along the road, just talkin' you know. We were bare footed, you know, never had no shoes on back in those days because it was nice and warm you know.

We came to a little muddy spot in the road where the cars and horses had gone across, and it made deep hoof prints down in that mud. The rains we had a couple days ago filled up all those hoof prints. It looked nice and clear. I said "Oh gee those hoof prints look nice and clear. That water looks good and clear, I'm gonna take me a drink." Pete and the boys they just stopped and looked at it with the mosquitoes flying on top of it. I brushed those mosquitoes away; I went down on my knees and took a long swallow. Phew! I spit it out. "How'd it taste? How'd it taste?" I made a face, "Terrible! It's warm and it tastes like pee!" Of course they didn't want to try it.

Well, we figured maybe we'd find some farmhouse and get a drink of water. So we kept on goin'. We came to another patch of berries and oh, we picked. Now our bucket was getting full, full up to the top. So we kept on walkin'. "Hey where we at?" We looked around, everything looked so different. We had never been there before. We came to the top of a hill and looked down in the valley, and there was a brickyard way down in the valley. "Gee, there's a brickyard down there, it's kind of strange though, it doesn't look like the Waynesburg brickyard. I wonder where we're at?" So we followed that road to a woods where three or four men were burning a home. "Let's ask those men where we're at." So we went up to those guys who were burning this home and I said "Say, you know where we're at? We're from Waynesburg and we're lost." "Waynesburg? You're a long way from home boys. You're in Malvern."

Malvern! Gee whiz, we started east and we ended up west. He said, "That's right. Just follow that road boys, you'll come to a place called P & M brickyard." From then on we knew where we were. We knew where P & M was because we had been there before. So we went down there, and here was a woman pumping some water. They had two little company homes, smaller than what we had up on the hill. And we stopped there for a drink of water.

"Hey you boys!" she recognized us. Her name was Gina, she used to live up on the hill. When she got married, they moved down to P & M. Her husband worked there. She asked, "What are you boys doing?" "Picking berries." "Yea I see that. Your mother will be proud of those berries, boy they're beautiful. She can make a lot of jam out of those." So we cupped our hands, and got a good drink of water.

We were hungry, but we didn't want to ask her for something to eat. So we said "Ok, goodbye we'll see you." We walked down the road, came to the railroad track and we followed the railroad track all the way into Waynesburg. We knew it would go right into town. Ben kept laggin' behind. "C'mon Ben, hurry up!" Here the reason he was walkin' so slow was because he was eatin' the blackberries! His nose was already pink and his mouth had blackberry stains on it. I said "Ben don't eat all those blackberries. Take 'em home for mom, she's gonna make some jam." Ben whined, "Well I'm hungry, I wanna eat some." I said, "Well don't eat 'em all." So we kept on walkin'. He kept laggin' behind, laggin' behind.

So we finally came to the Waynesburg brickyard, the one we were familiar with. We passed the old swimming hole but we didn't go in because we were tired. And we walked and finally reached the hill. Pete said, "Well Vic, we'll try it again someday." I said, "Yea maybe next week. We'll go back to a different place, I'm afraid of that dog up there." We said goodbye, then I went home. My mother saw that big bucket of blackberries. "Oh what beautiful berries! Boy, I'll make a lot of jam." We said "Ben's got a big bucket too."

When Ben came up there, my mother said, "How much you got Ben?" She looked, and his bucket was empty! He ate every doggone last berry. My God he ate 'em all! "Aw, I was hungry mom." My mother didn't say nothing to him. His face, heh, heh, you could have laughed. His face from his nose, all over his cheeks and down his chin was completely blue with blackberry stains. Boy I wanna tell you he looked like a clown, heh heh. It makes me wanna laugh. He used to have big, fat, chubby cheeks. He ate every one of those berries. So then mom told him to go wash his face, and we went in lookin' for something to eat.

I'll come back later on.

Chapter 3.

School Days

There are three stages of a man's life:
   1. *He believes in Santa Claus.*
   2. *He doesn't believe in Santa Claus.*
   3. *He is Santa Claus.*

Author Unknown [5]

Growing up as a boy, I had my share of bumps and bruises. I remember one day coming out of school and there was a big hay wagon going down the road. On the bottom of the truck there was a kind of low 2 by 4 that I knew I could sit on and ride. So I said "I'm gonna stick my head in the hay and sit on that 2 by 4, and I'm gonna ride it." So I plowed my head in there, and wouldn't you know I hit this one rod which was the brake. It didn't have the wooden handle on, it must have dropped off or something.

Anyhow I got poked right in the eye, it nearly knocked my eyeball out. And oh, didn't I have a bad eye. I went home, and my eye was all bloodshot and red. I went to the doctor, and I had a patch over that eye for a month. I really was in terrible pains.

Another time early in the spring, I wanted to pick some flowers to bring to school for the teacher. Down by the railroad tracks where we lived there were deep weeds and flowers. Like I said, we always went barefooted in the summer. I went down there and stepped on a big, broken beer bottle. It was lying down long ways. When I stepped on it, I got a cut from my toe all the way back to my heel, slashed clear across. And oh, did it bleed, and I was crying. I crossed my legs, and I held my foot with my two hands and the blood filled all the crease of my pants.

Some of the boys ran up "Victor got hurt, Vic got hurt." I'll never forget the big, heavy stocky woman that came down there. She picked me up in her arms, took me over the hill, across the railroad tracks and across to where we lived. And we had to call Dr. McCormick. My foot

---

5   Author Unknown

was wrapped up in a towel and bleeding all over the place. Mother was crying. So Dr. McCormick came with his horse and buggy. He said "Well, I'll have to put in stitches."

You didn't go to the hospital back in those days, and they didn't use nothing to numb it either. So what they did I'll never forget. They made a neighbor girl named Edith Mann sit on my lap to hold me down. The doctor took a long, curvy needle and long thread. He took the sponge, and I don't know what he used but it burned. He took this needle and he was sewing my foot like a cobbler would sew leather onto a shoe. In and out he pulled the string through and poked the needle on one side and poked through the other side and pulled the thread through. He did this until he stitched up my foot. And the whole time I was hollerin' and cryin'.

Edith, she felt sorry for me, "Poor Vic, poor Victor. You're always getting hurt." They had my foot propped up in a sling. And I never forget we had boarders at our house, and they came in to see me "Hey, how are you today?" Of course they talked to me in Italian, you know we always spoke Italian. *"Come ti senti oggi?"* It means *"How do you feel today?"*

But if that wasn't enough, the following summer we went down to the brick yard, we always went down to the brick yard to play, you know. Kids were throwing pieces of broken tiles and wouldn't you know I got hit smack in the eye that I had hurt a year or so before on that wagon. Again I had this eye bloodshot and I wore a patch over my eye for quite a while.

I have a story to tell you about one day when we were in school. They were giving a demonstration against smoking. Back in those days they said smoking wasn't good for you because it contained nicotine. They said tests were made where they put nicotine into a mouse's mouth, and in a short time the mouse died. I told the teacher, "Well, we have a cat at home that eats grasshoppers." The teacher exclaimed "What?" I said "Yes, we have a cat at home that eats grasshoppers." The teacher blinked, "Oh no, a cat doesn't eat grasshoppers. Those are insects. Cats don't eat insects, they eat meat." I said "Well, our cat does." The teacher shook her head, "I don't believe it." I insisted "You want me to bring it in tomorrow and show you?" She smiled "Well, yea, that would be interesting. But I don't think it will eat 'em."

So we went home that from night from school. Of course we didn't have to look very far for grasshoppers. Right in back of our house there's kind of a field with bushes. There were grasshoppers there, and they were hoppin' around. It was a nice, warm day and they were hoppin' from limb to limb. We would grab 'em with our hands. We had a jar, and we pulled their hind legs out so they couldn't jump away. So they just would walk, they couldn't hop.

We used to put 'em in the palm of our hands and say "Spit, spit!" And when we looked at our hands there would be a yellow spot there, like saliva. Well we used to do that quite a bit, make 'em spit, see.

So we collected, oh about a half a jar full, nice, big ones you know. We put the lid on and punched holes on top so they wouldn't die.

The next morning, we took our big cat. You know, of course we always had plenty of cats around. We had plenty of cats and dogs. So we took this cat to school. This time my brother, Herman, he went along. So at recess we went outside. The teacher called "Well c'mon." The class was kind of laughing at these dumb Italians. "They don't know what the heck they're talkin' about, whoever heard of a cat eating insects!" Well we felt comfortable, we weren't embarrassed. We knew what our cat could do.

So we went outside and word got around the class. Aww, we had practically the whole school gathered. They formed a big circle around us. Of course the cat was hungry at the time, you know. We kept it in a little sack so the cat hadn't eaten anything. The poor thing was hungry. We knew for sure he was gonna eat more than one. So we took the cat out of the bag and stroked it you know. And the cat stayed there and purred, you know how the cats go between your legs and purrs.

So we took these grasshoppers and we put one or two down. Boy that cat pounced on them and ate those grasshoppers. We put another one down, and he ate it. The teacher was shocked, "Oh my God, I've never seen a thing like that. You must starve that cat for it to eat grasshoppers." We said "No, it catches mice. We don't starve it, it catches mice." So the demonstration was over.

I remember going to school, and we used to recite poetry. Oh, I used to love some of that poetry. The teacher used to call on the different children to recite a verse or two of it, and I used to love it. It goes:

> *It was between the dark and daylight, when the night begins to lower, come a pause in the day's occupation that is known as the children's hour.*
> *I hear in the chambers above me, the patter of little feet, the sound of doors that are opened, and the voice soft and sweet.*
> *From my study I can see in the lamplight, descending the broad hall stair, grave Alice and laughing Allegra, and Edith with golden hair.* [6]

(This was in Victor's words from his memory of the famous poem <u>The Children's Hour</u> by Henry Wadsworth Longfellow. Victor's memory only adjusted a few words from the actual poem. Amazing!)

I used to love that. There's more to it but I'm not gonna recite it.

Then there was *The Village Blacksmith*. I used to love that because we had a village blacksmith here in town in little Waynesburg. Our wagon used to break, and we used to take it down there to have it repaired, you see. He would say "You boys are always breaking this wagon." His name was Derringer, and he lived down there by his shop. Oh, I remember when he put the iron into the fire, and he'd pull a handle and that handle would make air and that fire would glow, you know, and get red hot. Then he'd take that iron, and he would put in on the handle, *clink clank, clank clank, clink clank, clank*. The beautiful noise of the anvil. You know, the sound of the hammer striking. He would hit that hammer in rhythm, and he would repair our wagon. We used to watch him.

---

6 The Children's Hour by Henry Wadsworth Longfellow.

Then the farmer would come in there with the horse to be shoed, oh that was something. He'd put on a big, black leather apron, and he would take this horse's hoof and put it between his knees. He'd take a knife and first he'd pull out the old shoe, you know. Then he'd take a knife and he'd scrape that horse's hoof. Then he'd take a horseshoe, put it in the fire and get it red. He'd get it nice and hot you know, and he'd pound that to the shape of the horse's hoof. Pound that, put it in cold water, *shish,* you know to get it cold. Then he'd put that shoe on that horse. Oh, it was picture perfect.

Then he's put four or five nails in his mouth and he'd get that horse's leg again. He'd hold it between his knees and he'd take those nails again and bend 'em over on the other side and it was a beautiful thing to see. I loved the way the anvil would make that noise, I can still hear it today, and that's why I always liked that poem about the village blacksmith. It goes like this:

> *Under a spreading chestnut tree, the village smithy stands; the smithy a mighty man is he, with large and sinewy hands;*
> *And the muscles of his brawny arms are strong as iron bands.*
> *His hair is crisp and black and long, his face is like the tan; his brow is wet and honest sweat, he earns whatever he can,*
> *He looks the world in the face for he owes not any man."* [7]

(Again recited from memory with only a few words adjusted from the original poem <u>The Village Blacksmith</u> by Henry Wadsworth Longfellow!)

That was beautiful. So that was some of the things that we did.

Then in winter on school days, we would put on our clothes and shawl around our neck. It was cold you know, and we'd wind our way to school. Beautiful snow outside, and we would be in a room with a radiator on the back. I used to go on the back of that radiator and get warmed up you know, and then take my place in my seat. We would start with *I Pledge Allegiance to the Flag*. Then we would sing *America*.

---

7   The Village Blacksmith by Henry Wadsworth Longfellow

Then teacher would open one verse of the Bible. Yes, we read the Bible in those days, and the whole class said a prayer. Then we would start the class with a song. Oh, we would sing those songs you know. Beautiful songs. I still remember one that we used to sing. I won't attempt to sing it, but I'll just tell you the words, it goes like this:

> *"I know the song that the bluebird is singing, out in the apple tree where he is swinging.*
> *Brave little fellows the sky may be dreary, nothing cares he while his heart is so cheery.*
> *Listen awhile I'll tell you what he's saying, daffodils, daffodils say do you hear?*
> *Summer is coming and springtime is here."* [8]

That's the way that song went and I never forgot it.

(This is in Victor's words from his memory of the song <u>The Bluebird's Song</u> by Emily Huntington Miller with minor changes from the actual song!)

And of course we used to recite poetry *The Barefoot Boy* and *The Village Blacksmith* and things like that, that I enjoyed. And I loved to learn a little bit of history about our country. I learned about it more in later years by going to the library and reading more about the 48 states. After the 5th grade I quit school to go to the mine. But they made me go back, cuz I wasn't of age. I went back to school through the 6th grade, then that's all the schooling that I had.

When I was young, I was a very much misunderstood boy. Nobody would understand me. I didn't talk much. The reason for that was, I didn't know how it all started, but I used to stutter. In fact, I stutter a little bit yet, but not as bad as I used to.

Growing up as a boy I couldn't get my words started. The words used to get stuck in my throat, and I would try to speak but the words wouldn't come out. The only way I could speak clear and plain was if I talked loud and fast. By me talkin' fast, once I got started, I could get

---

[8] The Bluebird's Song by Emily Huntington Miller

goin'. But I just couldn't get goin'. One day we were in school, I'll never forget it must have been about the 2nd grade, my teacher's name was Helen McCormick. It was Dr. McCormick's daughter. She taught school there for many years. We would take the old McGuffey reader, good old McGuffey reader. She'd pick out a story, and what she used to do was call on one of the girls to start the story and we all had to pay attention to the book where she left off.

Then she'd have her sit down, and she'd call on a boy. He would pick it up where the girl left it off. Then she would tell him to sit down. Then she'd pick another boy, and he would pick it up. Then she finally would look back and she would call "Victor". I just froze. I just didn't want to talk, you know. I just knew that I would stutter, and they would make fun of me and I didn't want to be embarrassed. So I got up, and I knew my place. I stood there trying to make the words come out, but my throat was bulging, I was afraid to utter even a few words. I was afraid that I would stutter, and they would laugh at me. So I just stood there and stood there. The teacher said, "You lost your page. You're not paying attention. Sit down."

So this went on. It was embarrassing to me. Anyhow, I'd rather do that than start to talk and start stuttering. And I was very quiet. Outside playing I used to shout and holler. I didn't have the problem. But put me alone in a class when you had to talk easy and slow, I stuttered something terrible. Well the following day the same thing happened. She called on me, and I couldn't start talking. She'd make me sit down again.

Well this went on for a while. So when she finally called on me one day, we had the McGuffey Reader open to a different story. She had called different children up, and they all knew their place. She called "Victor." I got up, same as usual. I couldn't get my words out, afraid to speak that I would stutter and the children would laugh, call me dummy. I didn't want that, so I kept quiet pretending that I didn't know my place. I knew my place, I knew exactly where I was.

The teacher was mad. "You go out there in the hall." She made me go out in the hall, and she took her paddle. Well I went out in the hall and she said "What is it with you? Three times I called you and you're not paying any attention. She said everybody seems to know their place. Don't you know your place? Are you daydreaming? Is your mind wandering? What are you doing?" And I said "IIIII…" And I couldn't get it out. "III can't get started!" She said, "What do mean you can't get started, you don't want to start!" She was turning around, and she gave me a paddling. She never questioned me. I could tell her I was stuttering when I was alone and it wouldn't be so bad, but not in front of the class. It was too embarrassing. So that's the way that it was, always getting embarrassed that I stuttered.

I was coming back from school one day, as it started to rain. I was walking with one of the neighbor girls, Edith Delcorso. I said "Better hurry up, it's gonna rain" and we started walkin' kinda fast. And boy it started to hail. I never seen such big hail. Those hailstones hit us in the head, and oh my God it hurt. We covered up as best we could and we ran. She had nothing but a thin calico dress on. It was so wet it clung to her skin, and I was soaking wet. About halfway home we really got scared. It was lightning and thundering and that rain just came down in buckets. And those big hailstones, oh they would hit us. Edith got scared and started to cry. We both were so frightened. We ran and ran and ran. And we finally got home and changed into dry clothes. We didn't have enough sense to stop into a neighbor's home or get under a bush. We were anxious to get home.

One particular day we were at school, and they were having a campaign against rats. There were too many rats in the country so everybody was supposed to destroy rats because they were destroying grain and causing a lot of damage and even disease. So the school that would kill the most rats would get a prize. In order to prove that you killed the rats, all you had to do for each rat that you killed, was cut the tail off and bring the tails in a bag. That way they would know for how many tails you had would be how many rats, you see.

So I become a good rat killer. Now in our home in Waynesburg we had an oven outside where my mom baked bread with a roof up over the front of it so the loaves didn't get wet. The two sides were made out of tile. Now the tiles were from the brickyard, and they were open. There weren't corners you know, so you could look down into the two holes of the tiles and see clear through to the other side. The rats used to go in there and hide.

So I said, "Hey, let's go get some rats and get some tails." I told Herman "Take this big long pole and you poke on this side, I'll go on the other side. When the rat comes out I'll get him. So I went to the side. Boy when that rat came out, I got him. And that thing was just kind of biting you know, but I got him "Let's poke again." Two more rats came out. One got away, but I got the other one cornered. That thing, he showed his teeth. He got a hold of my shoe, we had big heavy soles, big shoes you know. This day I was wearing shoes, I wasn't goin' barefoot, Anyhow, that's how we got the rats.

Then we cut off their tails, we got three or four rats. Well, heh heh, what we did, we went down to the dump. In the back of the house where you throw your cans and stuff in the back of the house was a field, a kind of ravine. We would fill it up with garbage. Naturally there would be a lot of dead rats there that people would shoot or kill. Heh heh. We got us a stick and we're pokin' around in there. We cut off these dead rats tails. You know, heh, heh, heck we were supposed to get the rats alive and destroy 'em not get the ones that were already dead. But we wanted to show the amount of tails we could get, you see. So man I tell you we dug around there, and we went from dump to dump and house to house and we got a bag full.

And ohhhh we took 'em to school. The teacher was shocked, "Oh my gosh, how many rats did you get?" We were so proud! "Oh we got plenty of rats up there on the hill." Of course our dog Topsy was a good rat killer. He used to get the rat by the back of the neck and shake his head and kill 'em. But he wasn't around that day to kill rats for us, but he had done it on many occasions. But some of the rats Topsy had killed before were down in the dump, so we got those and cut off their tails. So and that's what we did we took 'em to school.

One year after our summer vacation was over and we went back to school, I came in late to class a couple of times. The teacher scolded me, "Now Vic, you're always coming in late. Can't you get here on time? The next time you come in here late I'm gonna put you in the dungeon." Now the dungeon was a place down in the cellar of the school on the girl's side. The West side was the girl's bathroom or toilet and the East was the boy's restrooms. And there was a big partition in between. Back in there was this dark dungeon with an iron gate. They kept a few little supplies in there, no lights or nothing. And everybody was afraid to go into the dungeon, because it was dark and oh, they were scared of the dark. The teachers would always threaten the boys and girls that if they did something wrong they would put 'em in the dungeon.

So when some of the kids did something wrong, they put 'em in the hall. One day the teacher said, "Vic go in the hall." I was talkin', you know. So I went out in the hall and stood. I was standin' in the corner of the hall, and there's a water fountain right there. I used to sneak over and take me a drink of water. Heck, if I'd a got caught I would get punished. I was being punished, I wasn't supposed to go there and drink any water but I did it, heh, heh. I went and got me a nice, cold drink of water. Then I went back in the corner. About ten minutes later, the teacher called me in.

We went on with our lessons till school was out, and we walked home. The next day, the same thing. We came into school, and I must have done something wrong. I don't remember what I did. But the teacher had enough. "Alright Victor, you're gonna go in the dungeon. You come in late, and you always get into mischief, so I'm calling Mr. Wagner." Now Mr. Wagner was our janitor who took care of the school. He rang the bell and fired the boilers in the wintertime. He also was our truant officer. If you played hooky, you knew he would pick you up, which he did one time I played hooky and he caught us.

Well, my teacher called Mr. Wagner, "I want you to take this boy and put him in the dungeon." He got me by the cuff of the neck, "All right you come with me." He dragged me outta that room you know, and I didn't wanna go. He just shoved me in front of him. Down the steps we went. He opened that big iron gate, put me in there and closed it. There I was in the dark all by myself. I looked around there, and I could feel with my hands some kind of tools and stuff, a wheelbarrow or something. I couldn't see. I was there about an hour, you know gee whiz, a long time. I had to go to the bathroom bad. So I thought "What am I gonna do? I'm not gonna wet my pants." So I went back there in the corner and I peed on something. I don't know what I peed on, but anyhow I did and I went all over the stuff that they had there. And of course I couldn't see it because it was dark. Then I went by the gate and looked out, and here it was recess. The bell was ringin' and all the kids came out to play. All the girls came down to go to the bathroom.

That's what you were supposed to do, go into the bathroom first, then go out to play. The girls from my room knew I was in there and started to peep into the gate lookin' in there, "Can you see him, can you see him?" I kept quiet, I didn't want them to know that I was there. And some of the girls from the other room said "Who's in there? Who's in there? Vic! Vic's in there. He's bein' punished, the teacher put him in the dungeon, Mr. Wagner put him in there. Where's he at? Where's he at?" So I thought I'd have myself a little joke on those kids, give em a scare. So they came close, cranin' their necks. I said "Boo!" They jumped back and screamed. They put their hands on their heads and they really got scared. Boy, I just stood there. I didn't laugh, never made a sound. Heh, heh, then the bell rang. Recess was over, and they went back to their rooms.

Now I could have snuck out of there because I opened that gate. There was a rope tying the gate and I could just squeeze thru. But I figured if I would have gotten out, I would get in worse trouble. I was in there a long time. I figured I might as well stay the rest of the day. Just before school was out, Mr. Wagner came and took me out. "Go back to your room." I went back to my room and the children were just putting all their books away. The teacher said "I hope this was a lesson for you now and you won't get into mischief again, or we'll put you back in there again." I didn't say a word. "All right, class is dismissed." We all got our coats and we made our way home.

One year my teacher's name was Miss Naylor. I always sat in the back of the class and us boys would always cut up, you know. I would take little paper wads and throw them. Well the teacher caught me throwing the paper wads and said "Victor come up here'. Why aren't you studying your lessons?" You see they had the class divided in half. One half of the room would be one grade and the other half of the room would be another grade. Well, she would teach one half of the class while this other half was supposed to be studying. She made me go up there, and she said "Get under my desk." Heh, heh, instead of standing in the corner, she put me under her desk.

At her desk she had a swivel chair that she would put in front of her desk where she would sit. She would talk from there, and sometimes she would stand and teach with a ruler in her hand and point to the board. Well this particular time I was stuck under the desk. She must have forgot about me because I was there a long time. When she finally sat down she crossed her legs. Of course back in those days the dress came down below her knees you know, kind of long. And it had all kinds of petticoats. I don't know why a woman back in those days wore so many petticoats. I bet she had about six or seven petticoats. I wanted to see how many petticoats she had on. Well I got the end of her skirt with my fingers real easy, not to make any movement you know. She had a white one and I think she had a blue one and then she had a black one and she had a pink one, and my gosh looks like I'll never come to the end. And here finally I turned the last one, a real fine silky one you know; oh I'll bet she had 4 or 5 on.

And she had big, black bloomers, you know. They weren't so long. Later on they used to call them bloomer girls, you know, when the girls got bold, they used to go around in their bloomers. No dress, just big black bloomers down to below their ankles and they called them bloomer girls. Well that's what they had, they didn't wear panties like what you have now. So I was there looking at all these petticoats, and she happened to move her leg, and she bumped me. She jumped up "Vic, you're under there yet, I forgot all about you!" She got embarrassed. She knew she crossed her legs, and she thought maybe I would see something. I didn't see nothing, just a bunch of petticoats. "Go back to your seat." So I went back to my seat and sat down. Before long the school day was over and we went home.

Well I messed up again. I drew a picture. I was no artist, but I tried to draw a cartoon of a woman the way I thought a woman would look you know. I tried to draw it in the nude. You couldn't tell any difference, I didn't know male and female back in those days, only what I saw on horses and cows. Heh, that's the only way I knew the difference between a boy and a girl. So I drew up a sketch of her and I put on there, Miss Naylor. Then I drew a sketch of our Professor, named Egan. I wrote on the top, Professor Egan loves Miss Naylor. I thought it was sort of a joke like, you know. From lookin' at it, it wasn't all that bad. Like I said I was no artist, nothing bad or indecent about it. We were innocent, didn't know anything. I didn't mean any harm by it.

This friend of mine, name was Edward, he busted out laughing. The teacher said, "What's so funny back there?" Edward told her "Oh, Victor drew a funny picture." She said, "Let me have it." I took it up there, and she opened it up. Her face blushed. The kids said, "What is it? What is it?" Miss Naylor looked at me and said to the class "Never mind. Victor you stay after school. The principal will take care of you." So that was the end of that. We had class and recess. When school let out that afternoon, all the kids went home, and there I was in my seat. And down comes Professor Egan.

He came down there, and they were in the corner talking. She showed him that paper, and he got the paddle. We had two paddles. We had a small one and a big one. Well, he took the big paddle. And I knew he would hit hard. The teacher would hit and hurt, but a man, he would hurt you more. So I was afraid. He came back there, and I got a hold of my seat. I held that seat so tight, he couldn't get me.

He put the paddle down, and he got both hands, and he got me by the shoulders. "Come here Vic." He almost pulled the seats up from the floor as he yanked me out. He pulled my pants up tight so he could hurt me more. And he threw me over that bench, bent me over the top of my desk and he took that paddle and oh, he walloped me. Oh my God it hurt. And Miss Naylor thought it was enough so she walked back there and said, "I think he had enough punishment." He must not like Italians or something because he paid no attention to her.

And he bent me back there again, and he started walloping me the second time. And it hurt, so I put my hands on the back of my butt. And he come with that paddle right across my four knuckles, knocked the skin out of my four knuckles. Oh, I screamed and he saw that he had hit my fingers. I jumped up and caught my left hand with my right hand, by the wrist. My fingers were bleeding, and he saw that. I imagine he probably got scared. The teacher said, "My Lord." And he said, "Why did you put your hands back there for?" That dummy, because it hurt, that's why. I didn't tell him that, but it hurt and I had to do something.

The teacher felt sorry for me, but he looked like he was enjoying it. So the teacher she wiped it off as best as she could. She said, "Go home, and get that bandaged." She was sorry it happened but said I shouldn't have put my hand back there. I was crying and sobbing.

I went home and showed my mother "What'd you do to your

hand?" I told her "I got a lickin." "What for?" "For nothing, I didn't do nothing." I lied, I didn't want to tell her I drew a picture of the teacher. "I didn't do nothing." That made my parents mad. There was a man up on the hill who could speak good English. He passed himself off as some kind of a lawyer. He wasn't a licensed lawyer, but he defended all the Italians that had any kind of problems or trouble. They would call him, and he would explain to the parents just what was going on in school.

So he went to school the following day under my father's orders, to tell the school that he resented what was done to his boy. He thought it was alright to give me a paddling but not to knock the skin off my fingers. So the neighbor man went there and they started talkin' I didn't hear what they were saying. They showed him the picture that I drew. He came back to me. "Did you draw this Vic?" I said "Yes." He asked "Do you know what this is?" I told him I didn't, I just thought it was funny. So when I got home he faced my dad. My dad said, "Doggone Vic, next time you'll learn not to do things like that at school." So he didn't hit me that time. He figured that I had enough at school, my hand was bandaged up.

❦

Well after that me and this teacher got to be the best of friends. We used to have an organ in there. We used to have to peddle it you know to let the air in. Then the air would blow and you could play, see. One of the straps that worked the peddle was broken. Gee that organ was broke, and they didn't repair it for a long time. Nobody was repairing it. So I went back there to see what I could do with it. And I noticed that there was a hook on that peddle and a hole in that big leather belt that would hook onto the peddle. It had come loose. I took that strap and pulled it down, and inserted it over the hole of the peddle. And it worked!

The teacher was so happy, "Oh you fixed it, what'd you do to it Vic?" I said, "Well there's a little hook there, and the strap is getting kind of old. The hole is a little bit too large. And once in a while when you pump you'll kick that strap off and it won't play." She was really grateful.

❦

Now when we were in school, we always went home for lunch. In nice weather they allowed us to bring a bucket, or as you would call it, a lunchbox. We used to pack our meals and eat downstairs in the boiler room. At least that's where the Italians, the guys from the hills, had to eat. Some of the better class of people got the privilege to eat right in the room but we couldn't do that. All of us people from the hill had to eat downstairs.

On this particular day we went home, and mom had sausage with garlic ready for us. We ate a lot of garlic. Aww, she put garlic in everything. And oh, was that sausage good. And she had potatoes and she'd have pizza pie, she'd have all different things for us to eat. When we went back to school, we'd play outside before the bell would ring. We would run you know and get all heated up. When we went in the room, well we were breathing kind of heavy see. When I sat in the seat naturally that garlic breath went to the kids on the front and on the sides of me. The girls, oh they would hold their nose. They would say, "Oh my God! You stink!" The teacher would say "Who's been eating garlic in here?" The girls would tell her, "Victor and these two boys here."

So the teacher came back there, and opened up all the windows. She said "Don't you ever eat garlic again. If you must eat garlic, eat it on Saturday when you don't have school. My God you're smelling up all the room." That was an embarrassment. We told mom, "Don't give us no garlic, because the teacher said it stinks." Mom said, "Aww, that teacher don't know what's good for you. That garlic ain't gonna hurt you". So she just wouldn't stop it.

Herman and I and a bunch of us always used to set traps to catch rabbits, groundhogs or whatever we could get. We would check our traps every morning to see what we caught. So this one particular morning Herman said, "Hey Vic, before we go to school, let's get up early and go check our traps. Let's see if we caught anything." So Herman and I we went down to the woods, about a mile away from where the school was.

We went there and looked at our traps, but we didn't catch anything. In one trap we just found a rabbit leg. See if you don't go there early enough, they will chew up their own leg to get away. So we lost that rabbit. When we came to the last trap we saw something bouncing around in there. Here it was a skunk. We were happy. "Oh, we got a skunk! We can sell that fur to make a good muff." So Herman, he goes up to the skunk to try to take it out of the trap. What we didn't know was the skunk could really make you stink, see.

So I was more to the side, and Herman went to get the trap and that skunk lifted up his tail and boy Herman got a shower. Ohhh he stunk. I got some on me too, but not as much as him. I stunk pretty bad too, but Herman got the worst of it. So we went on to school. Herman said "We'd better hurry or we're gonna be late". By the time we got to school, we kind of got used to the smell on us. We could smell it, but we didn't mind. We went into school and the kids were already in their seats with the teacher getting ready to start the lesson.

When we walked in that room, My God, everybody, heh heh, held their fingers to their nose, "Oh God! Skunk! You kids get out of this room, you're smelling it up!" The teacher opened up all the windows and yelled, "You get out of this room and go on home! Don't come back to school until you take a bath!" And so, heh, heh, me and Herman were embarrassed.

We went home and told our mother. We didn't have to tell her, she could smell it. She said, "What'd you boys do? My God!" Anyhow, she had to take the clothes off, she had to burn 'em. She burned em in the stove. She took this great, big, brown bar of soap and put us in the tub. Heh heh, she scrubbed and scrubbed and scrubbed us you know. Well, we didn't go back to school because we stunk so much. She put powder on us, and later on that night she gave us another bath. And I don't know what else she put on us. Anyhow she finally got us cleaned up so we could go back to school.

We'd get up every morning to beautiful sunshine. We'd walk through the woods, go through the meadow and hear the song of the whippoorwill, the meadowlark and robins. It was music to my ears. We'd run through the woods in the deep clover until we came down to the river. We'd wade and swim and do all those things in summer that a normal boy would do like swimming, fishing going through the woods, playing games, going to the barn or playing hide and seek. Then we'd make our way home after a long day in the countryside, walking barefoot into that soft sand that used to ooze through your toes. What a wonderful feeling! We would run, and we were happy. When we got home, our parents would be there.

I remember, oh we would sit around a long table, our dad, our sisters and all of our brothers. Mom used to make the supper. She had a great big pot. Whatever it was that she made started in that pot: pasta beans, pasta badad (a nasty mixture of potatoes, water and God knows what else), spaghetti, chicken soup, everything. We would all sit around that table, and we would eat. Some nights we didn't like the meals so much and dad used to say. "Well, you're not hungry. Put the pot back on the stove. When you get hungry it will be there, and it will taste good then." That was just the way it was. We'd go out to play some more around the neighborhood and when we came in, we were hungry. And then it was good!

We loved to go outside in the dark. The stars were shining so bright in the sky. We could see the Big Dipper and hear the sound of the crickets making their noise. It would start with a loud chirp and finally wind itself down. Then another one would start from a different tree and pick up that sound. The chirping of the insects, oh how I loved that beautiful country noise. Down from the river not far from our home the frogs would start their croaking. They would sing back and forth. One would start a deep croak then another one at a higher pitch and that would go on late into the night. I remember climbing up the stairs going to the 3rd floor where we slept, and lay in our straw mattress, two at the head and one at the foot.

By morning we'd all be rolled into the center because the mattress would form a hole in the middle. There were no curtains at the window. We could see the stars in the sky and the great big harvest moon going across our window. We would hear the sound of the crickets and the frogs croaking down at the river and in the ponds. Beautiful country sounds. I cherish those sounds.

To this day I love nature. I was a boy that loved nature. Everything from the smell of the new mown hay, to the sweet fragrance of all the flowers, the violets, daffodils and pussy willows. Early in the spring, I'd take them to school to our teacher.

Going to school around Christmas time was always a nice time and fascinating to me. We used to have teachers that knew how to draw with colored chalks. There was a blackboard on the south side of the wall and one in the front facing east. We didn't use that board as much, we always used the front board so the class could look straight ahead while the teacher would write.

She used to paint a beautiful winter scene using all kinds of colors, she was really an artist. She painted a beautiful farmhouse with a lane going to it with lights shining inside of the windows. Then there was a rail fence along the side with a little squirrel perched on top of a post and an open sleigh with a horse going through this here lane. The sleigh was loaded with happy people, scarves around their necks, big bundles of presents tied on back on the sled, and this horse with a bell tied around the middle. It was called *"Over the River and Through the Woods to Grandmother's house we go."* That's what she painted. She painted that scene. And it was so beautiful.

And I never forget how we sang Christmas songs, *"Joy to the World," "Hark the "Herald Angels Sing," "Silent Night,"* all those beautiful hymns. We had no classes so it was kind of a treat for us. She would say, "Now Santa Claus is gonna come, Santa Claus is gonna come." We were all happy you know, wondering what we were gonna get. All the stores in Waynesburg would donate stuff, popcorn, little candies, small things like that.

Then Santa Claus would come laughing in his merry way,"Ho, Ho Ho!" He had a white beard, a jolly looking fellow. We were just thrilled. We were lookin' and sayin', "Santa Claus, Santa Claus" And he would call row by row. We would go up, and he would hand us a red sock. It had a big popcorn ball in there, a big orange on the top, hard rock candy down into the bottom and a little candy train. A wee little candy, almost the size of jelly beans, small, except they were round. Some were black, some were white some were red and it was a nice little train. And each one of us got a stockin'.

We were so happy. We held that stockin' you know. I remember we sang Christmas songs. Santa would leave our room and go to the different rooms. We had a little Christmas tree in the corner made with homemade ornaments. We would take papers and make them into a chain. Some were white, some were green, some were blue. We would draw different things and hang 'em on the tree. Of course back in those days we would use candles, we didn't have electric lights. And that's the way we would have our Christmas. Then we would wind our way home and show our parents what we got at school. Then we were off for Christmas vacation.

When we got home, our mother was preparing the Christmas meal. I remember we always had a wonderful Christmas meal. She had chicken made up in four or five different ways and there was always wedding soup. Oh she fixed the table beautiful. At night we would all hang our stockings, big long black stockings. We used to wear these pants called knicker pants that used to come up to our knees. We didn't wear long pants back in those days. We had these big, long, black stockings and pants that came up to our knees like some of the golfers used to wear called knickers. That's what us boys wore. The girls wore dresses. And we would hang those black stockings up on the door of the cold kitchen stove. All our stockings would be hanging there. We knew Santa Claus was gonna come the next day, and our parents gave us a little treat.

We'd hustle up to our bed on the third floor. It was cold, the snow was blowing. We had no curtains or blinds on the window, and the snow used to come in from the cracks around the window frame. It was just a 2 by 8 frame of wood. Naturally you could see the daylight from outside. If the wind was blowing the right way, it used to blow in there at the foot of our bed. There used to be snow in there, actual snow. We had no fire in the house, we never kept a fire in the house until we got the big pot belly stove. But that came later.

We slept in our long underwear like long johns. We had no pajamas, just long johns. In the morning we would all go downstairs to find all our stockings filled. What we would find in our stockings was a big hunk of black coal, a little orange, some cane candy and hard rock candy, with red and blue stripes around it. We used to get some loose change, a dime, or a nickel or some pennies up to a quarter. Now a quarter was a lot of money. I remember I used to go downtown with that quarter and go to some kind of a store. They had toys, beautiful toys made of cast iron, and I bought me something for a quarter. And we were really happy.

Then came the meal on Christmas Day. It was served on the table, and we would all sit down and eat that wonderful meal that mom used to make. We had a wonderful time. And that's the way we spent our Christmas.

Bye for now.

Chapter 4.

Life in Waynesburg, Ohio

Directly after God in heaven comes papa
                    W. A. Mozart (1756-1791) [9]

It's me again. I thought I'd come back to a few more of my boyhood days in Waynesburg, Ohio. While we lived in Waynesburg, my sister Jenny was born. She was the last to be born. Of course Ben, Lawrence and Johnny were also born there. We lived in a different house now. Remember Edith Mann? That's the girl who used to feel sorry for me every time I got hurt or got a lickin'. She used to always take up my side and feel sorry for me. Well her family moved, closer to town and we moved from the old house on the hill into their home which was just down below. We spent the remaining time in Waynesburg in that particular home.

This one particular summer day, a bunch of us boys from the hill and of course all the dogs, Topsy, Butch and I don't remember the rest of the dog's names headed for the woods. One dog followed and then all the dogs from the hill would naturally come along whether we called them or not. They just knew they were going out to the woods, and that was a treat for them. So along the railroad tracks was a line of box cars, you know for the brick yard to load. We used to go on top of those box cars, and run the whole top of 'em. You'd run a while and then there would be a gap in between. We used to take a flying run and jump one boxcar to the other. We always would make it. Of course the smaller kids were afraid. They would climb down one car and come up the next car until we'd come to the end. Then we would get off and walk down to where we would go to swim.

But this time we went swimming in a different place. We didn't go to our old swimming hole. It seemed to be a little rapid there. The river was divided in two parts like there was an island in the middle, a small island, and then there was a rapid on one side. And I couldn't swim.

---

9   W. A. Mozart (1756-1791)

So that day I was swimming there, and I got caught in that rapid. The faster I'd swim, the more the water would take me down. Awww, I was swallowing water and I was drowning. I couldn't holler. My friend, Pete Vinci noticed that. He jumped in, picked me up, took me out and tapped me on the back. I was coughin' and oh my gosh, he said I really coughed up water. And that scared me from swimming. You know I don't think I went swimming very much after that. It kind of scared me. I nearly drowned. It wasn't so deep, but the water ran down a bunch of rocks and was really swift.

Another time there was a big wall right by our house with a great big plank lying across it. I used to walk on that plank and it would rock like a see saw. And each time I'd go a little bit further, then I'd run back. Then I'd go a little bit further, I thought it was fun, then I'd run back. So this one time I went a little bit too far and down went the big heavy plank and down I fell into a bunch of tin cans and rubbish and stuff and knocked myself completely out.

The first thing I remember was my mother carrying me in her arms. She took me in the house where I came to. But the worst I got there was the wind knocked out of me and a lot of cuts and bruises. I didn't break a bone. I was lucky that big plank didn't fall on top of me, it would have crushed me.

I had many, many experiences. As a kid in summertime I put my hand into a knot of an apple tree to pull out a birds nest, and here a snake put up his head. My gosh I jumped! That snake used that knot hole for a nest.

Another time it was a fine summer morning and all us boys would get up and say, "What are we gonna do today? How about, let's go fishing?" So we took our big fishing pole. They weren't cane poles, they were made from a big branch of a tree, you know. We just chopped a big, long branch off. Then we'd take a wire, put a hook on it, dig some worms and we'd go fishing.

The fishing hole was deep with a lot of sunfish in there. So we'd fish awhile. Aww, it was one of those days when the fish weren't biting. We kind of were fooling around there and looking for something to do. There was a railroad track nearby with a big culvert that went across the track. It had stagnant water on one side and it was full of weeds. They looked like palm leaves, you know sticking up from the water. And we noticed snakes in there.

"Oh hey, let's go catch some snakes!" We had our dog, Topsy, along as usual, and boy he could catch snakes better than anything that I knew, outside of rats you know. He could catch a lot of rats too. And Topsy would go in there, and he would get that snake by the neck, give him a couple twists and then the snake would soon die. We'd get 'em and throw 'em on the lawn on a grassy spot.

So we took some homemade clubs and rolled up our pants. We were wading through those weeds and we'd spot one. "There's one, there's one!" Bang! We'd hit those snakes, and we'd get 'em you know. "I got one! I got one!" All of us kids were wading through there, moving those palm leaves aside. We'd see one squirming away and Bang! We'd hit it and get 'em. And oh I bet we caught about 25 of 'em. We looked around for more, but we didn't see anymore. Of course we knew there was a lot more in there, but they must have run up further. So we got tired of that and we said "What are we gonna do with all these snakes?"

Well I got an Idea. "Hey, why don't we put 'em all across the railroad track and wait when the train comes to cut 'em all in half." So that's what we decided to do. We took all those snakes, about 25 of 'em, maybe more. We heard a freight train coming. "Here comes the train!" And the engine and the whole load of boxcars, coal cars and finally the caboose went by. We rushed up to the track and there they were. Half of the snakes were on one side of the track, and half on the other side. Oh, we took our cane and we put 'em all over the cane like you would hang sausage to dry. We hung all those snakes on this long fishing pole of ours, you see.

And then we put one end on my shoulder and the other end on another boy's shoulder and I said "Hey, let's take these here snakes home and scare the girls up on the hill." Remember we called it the hill, also known as bedbug row. All of the houses are one after the other. So we went up there real proud. We went right smack to the front of the houses where people usually sit under their porch. And oh those girls saw those snakes, "Oh my gosh, get away from me!" We went towards the girls with those snakes dangling from that fishing pole. The mothers said, "You take those snakes away from here! What's a matter you boys, you crazy? Take 'em away from here!" They took brooms after us, and they started chasing us with their brooms.

So we went way behind the field, in back of the houses. There's nothing there but empty fields and beyond that the railroad track and then the river. We ran toward this embankment and threw the whole thing up over the embankment. That's how we got rid of the snakes. Oh, we had such fun as that.

We had a little grocery store, and we had to deliver groceries sometimes clear on the other end of town. I had a little two-wheel wagon that I built with two wheelbarrow wheels and a big box on top. So me, Pat and Herman, took this wagon and we delivered all these groceries. On the way back we were walking down the sidewalk. Herman decided he wanted to ride. He said "Push me." I told him "No, we're tired."

He got in the wagon anyway and here we had to push him, me and Pat. We had a hold of the handles in front and we were just pulling this wagon and there he was in the back there, ridin'. So we come across this here bridge. There's kind of a little creek there with a high bank where the road would be and a steep bank on the side with a slope. It would slope down to this here brook. Now the brook at that time was pretty high because the rains we had the day before kind of made the river higher than what it usually is. So we said "Let's throw him down that embankment."

So me and Pat turned the handle around and gave the wagon a shove. Down the embankment the wagon rolled. My gosh, he could have tipped over, fallen into the river and drowned. It went straight down and hit some deep grass about two feet short of going into the river. And it stopped. Boy he got mad. He said "All right, you guys threw that wagon down there, now you guys take it out." We said "No, you gotta help, the wagon's too doggone heavy." He stomped off "You pushed it down there, you take it out" and he started walkin' home. So Pat and I, we went down there, and we tugged and pushed and tugged and finally got it out and took the wagon home. And Herman never said a word. One thing about him, he never squealed. He didn't say, "They threw me in the river." Heh, heh, that's what he gets for ridin'.

Another time my dad bought an old horse. Oh was that horse old. The bones were sticking out on him, and he was supposed to pull the wagon now that business was getting better. So we were supposed to deliver some groceries to Magnolia. Every time we had to go through Magnolia, there were these young guys sitting on the square. They would holler "Ho Nellie! Ho Nellie!" and that old horse would stop. And boy that would embarrass us. "Get up! Get up!" That horse wouldn't move. We'd hit it with the reins and say "Get up! Get up!" They'd joke and laugh, and boy we were embarrassed.

The following week we had to take a trip back there again. When we came to the square of Magnolia, Herman said "You guys drive the horse through town, I'm gonna walk around these back alleys and I'll meet you on the other side of town." Heh, heh, he didn't wanna go through the street where those guys were. So this horse was going down there, and the young guys were there again. They pulled the same old trick. "Ho, Ho, Ho there, Ho there Nellie, Ho there." Everybody called the horse Nellie, I don't know why. But they said "Ho Nellie, Ho Nellie" and the old horse would stop.

So I got off and got the horse by the bridle and I led him out of town. And we got by. On the way back home, Herman again would say he's meet us at the other end of town. He'd be waiting there and would jump on the wagon. He did the same thing coming back, he'd walk around town. When we went through town that time, the young fellas weren't there so we didn't get embarrassed again.

Well it started to rain. And, oh my gosh we wanted that horse to go but he wouldn't move. The clouds were getting dark, and it was thundering. We knew it was gonna be a big shower. "Get up there!"And the horse would go a couple feet clip-clop, clip-clop, just as slow as Moses. So I jumped off and picked up a picket stick. You know those sticks that are used to make picket fences? I pulled one of those out, and I got that stick and I was hitting that horse on the back, Whang! Whang! Then some woman came up and said "Hey, you stop hitting that old horse! I'll have you arrested."

Well, we got scared and threw that stick away so doggone fast and sat there without raising our heads. And that old horse was just going as slow as heck. I didn't mean to hurt that horse, it was just so frustrating. We were drenched to the bone when we got home. And that's the kind of embarrassment we had to take.

One night about 10:00 PM we got an order for some of mom's bread. Some fellow wanted two loaves. It was dark, and in those days there were no street lights. Pat and I had the job to deliver, so we took those loaves of bread in the bag, and we went down the street. Oh it was dark!

On the other side of the street, all you could see was the shadows of homes. We were going down this hill to a place called 'The Flat,' another row of block houses that belonged to the company. We were walking along and there wasn't a sound to be heard. All at once we hear a kind of moan, 'Whoaaaa.' Oh my gosh, we stopped still, but couldn't figure out what it was that scared us. It went again 'Whoaaaa.' I thought it was a cow since there was a barn nearby. We kind of laughed "That's a cow, that's a cow." So we crossed over the railroad tracks down below the flats, delivered the bread and came back home. We never did find out for sure what had made that noise.

Now don't any of you grandchildren do any of the things I did when I was a boy. It would fill up a book if I could just remember it all. Back in my day, it was different. There was no TV, no radio or any of the things you have today. We made do with what we had, going into the woods looking for chestnuts, hunting mushrooms and swimming. In the winter we'd go to the pond by the brick yard by the kiln where they cook the bricks and we'd get warm.

Now it was always me who was getting hurt. But this time I have something to say about my brother, Ben. One day while living up on the hill, we got up from our third floor bedroom where we used to sleep on our straw mattress. We'd go down to the first floor, have a big bowl of black coffee and bread. That was our breakfast. In those days we didn't have any cereals. So a big bowl of black coffee with a little sugar in it was our breakfast.

So after we got that done we would go outside and see what we could do for the day. We'd walk up to the top of the hill to this here watershed that had a flat roof. There were water meters inside. We'd used to sit on top of there. All the boys used to come up and gather. Pete Vinci and his brother Albert and Ben and a few other boys, and we'd say "What should we do? Should we play some kind of a game?" So we decided to play the game *Kick the Can*.

We went home and got a broomstick. When the brooms were kind of worn out, we'd cut off the old broom and use the handle for a stick. We left the hill, and all of us kids had these broomsticks in our hand. Then we chose sides. We took an old tomato can, and we'd hit that can in the air. Boy that can would sail up in the air, go way up, back and forth. Oh the fun we'd have.

That can would get all battered up, so we'd change cans and get a new can and start the game over again. I don't know who did it, but some boy instead of hitting the can up in the air he hit it straight and it hit my brother, Ben, right smack in the nose, right on the bridge of his nose. Oh he cried, and blood came out of his nose. I remember taking my brother, Ben, and I was holding his nose with blood running through my fingers. There was blood all over. I took him home and mom said "Vic, Vic what'd you do? What am I gonna do with you?" "Mom I didn't do anything. It was an accident, we were playin' *Kick the Can* and he got hit in the nose with a can." My mother washed him you know, and stopped the blood. Oh he had a sore nose for a long time.

What we didn't know at the time was that he had actually broken that bone on his nose, and shut the one side of his nostril. Now he only could breathe on one side of his nose. He could breathe through it some, but not so much. Years later when he had to sign up for the draft, he went for a physical. The doctor asked him, "Have you hurt your nose at one time or another? He said "Yea, when I was a kid, I got hit with a tin can."

Well, he had broken his nose and the one nostril healed shut. The doctor said, "You're gonna have to go to a doctor to drill up there and open up that nostril so you can breathe on both sides." So that's what he did. He had to have surgery and cut that there opening through his nose that was plugged. Now today he breathes normal. Those were the kinds of games we played when we were boys.

I'm gonna tell you about my little baby (sister) Jenny when she was small. Mom used to nurse her. I remember one time when mom was busy workin', getting supper and washin' clothes. Little Jenny would be cryin', she wanted to eat. Mom would stop her work and take my baby Jenny, my sister, and she would put her on her lap. She would take out her breast, and in those days it was common to see women nursing their babies. It wasn't like today kids might make jokes out of it. It was a natural thing you know, we took it for granted that was the way babies were fed.

So this day my mom was nursing my little baby, Jenny, and we would go up close to my sister. Those little dark eyes would turn around and look up at us you know and kind of smile and stop sucking. The milk would run down the side of her mouth. Mom would say "Now you boys leave her alone! I've got work to do! I want to feed her so she can go back to sleep so I can do my work." So we would just stay there and keep looking at the baby, and the baby would keep looking at us. So what mom would do is she would take her breast out of the baby's mouth, and she would squeeze it, and squirt us in the face. That milk would come in our face, and we would jump back and rub our eyes and naturally she would start nursing the baby again. Then we would leave the house.

We'd take a walk up the row of homes toward where our friends lived. We'd pass house after house and see all the mothers outside sitting in their chairs nursing their babies. We didn't think anything of it. It was a natural thing. We came to this one woman's house in particular. She lived about four or five houses above us. Her name was Carlotta. She was a big, stout woman. She wasn't a fat woman, but she was built big, strong and husky. She had a cute little baby. Carlotta was nursing her baby, and she had the biggest breasts that I'd ever seen. She would make Dolly Parton look sick. Of course I didn't know anything about Dolly Parton then. It is in comparison for me to tell you how she looked to me. Big.

Well we didn't pay attention to it, we just looked at the baby. The little baby's face was completely buried in the mother's breast and from time to time the mother had to lift up her breast with her one hand to expose the baby's nose so the baby could breathe and the baby wouldn't smother. Those are the kinds of things that we did to pass the time trying to find something to do for the day.

Now I'll tell you about Grandma and how she used to bake her bread when we lived in Waynesburg. She used these big outside ovens where she did her baking. When she finished her baking, she'd load the ovens with wood so the wood would get nice and dry. Then the next time she baked her bread the wood would catch on fire easy.

She had a great big bread box. Oh, it was as big as a baby's crib. It was narrow on the bottom and got wider up the side. We used to buy 100 pounds of flour at a time. It was called the *4X Flour*. Mom would take about half of that box of flour and put yeast in there, and mix this here dough. She would knead it and knead it, you know, and cover it up and wait for it to rise. When it would rise up to the top, she would punch it down and cover it up again. Then she would go out and light her fire and get the oven going. By the time the bread was done, the oven would be ready to bake.

She used to put paper in there to light the fire. When the crown of that oven got real white, then you knew the oven was ready. From time to time she checked to see if the dome of the oven was white and ready to bake. She would go back in the house to punch the dough down for the second time, and when it would rise up again, she'd take a lot of that dough and put it on the table. I remember mom would cut it, and make big loaves of bread, like big cart wheels. She used to make 21 loaves at a time. Of course mom sold the bread too.

She had big long boards, and she would put the dough on there and cut it. All 21 loaves would be on the boards, and she'd wait for the loaves to rise. While the dough was rising, she would go out and rake all the ashes out of the oven. The oven would be all white and ready to bake. She'd pull all the ashes out with a long scraper, and then she'd take a damp mop. She'd go in there and mop the floor of this here oven. Then she'd take all the ashes out and pick up all the dirt and the dust so the bread would be clean. Then when that was all ready she'd go in the house and take these long boards with the bread on them and take them out to the oven. She'd use these big scoops, long handled, shovel-like things, and put each loaf of bread on there to put it into the oven. Then she'd give it a little pull and pop the bread in place. She would line 'em in there real nice and neat.

She used to have some dough left, and she would make two big pizza pies. She used all the fat from the lard that we melted when we butchered our hogs. She saved all the little pieces of meat that were left after frying out all the lard and kept them in a crock. So she'd take a handful or two of these bits of meat and spread it all over the dough and knead it in there the same way you'd put raisins into bread to make raisin bread. We called them chickers, little chickers, little pieces of meat. Then she'd take these two big pizza pies and put a little bit of oil and a little bit of salt and pepper on the top. She would put these two pies right in front of the oven, and close the oven. When the bread was done, oh that would smell good! She would pull out the pizza pies and put them aside. She'd take out the bread and tap them on the bottom and lay them on this board and take them into the house.

Mom used to sell the bread. She had this great big bread box where she stored it. We sold some and kept enough for the family. Then it was time to eat. And oh, when we cut that pizza pie! It was thick, not thin like you buy now. It was real thick. And when you bit into it, oh was that delicious! My mouth is still watering now. I wish I had a piece of that old time pizza.

When it was time for us to go to bed at night, we went upstairs to the third floor. Our mattress was stuffed with straw, and we would jump in the bed and cover up to keep nice and warm. My mother always kept a chamber pot for us to pee in at night. She kept it in the corner of the room and we always had a kerosene lamp there. We always wanted a light in there because it was very dark. It was too cold outside to go to the outhouse, so my mother would have this pot for us to go in.

We had boarders that slept in the next room. During the night the boarders were too lazy to get dressed and go outside to the outhouse. They used to do their business in our pot. So one night, I got up during the night and I had to go bad. I walked over to the pot, and it was full to the brim. Those boarders had used our pot until they filled it. And I had to go.

I didn't want to go on the floor so I had to do something. There were some boots sitting there. The boarders worked in the mine and their rubber boots were sitting there. I took one of those boots and I peed in that boot. That's what I did. I went back to bed and went to sleep. Well the next morning when that boarder got up, he put his stockings on, put his foot in that boot and awww he got a wet foot! His foot got wet, and he got mad. He went down and told my father, "Look what your boys did up there. They peed in my boot, look at my sock. It's all wet!"

So, my dad, right away, he suspected me, "Victor, come down here". So I went down there, "Why'd you pee in the boot for? You know better than that! Why didn't you use the pot?" "Pop, when I got to the pot it was full up to the brim. They had used it and filled it up, and there was no place for me to go. I had to go, so I peed in his boot."

My dad got mad. "You mean to tell me that you men are using the boy's pot? Why didn't you go outside and use the outhouse? I use the outhouse when I have to. You guys are no better than me." He said "I don't blame you for peeing in the boot, I would have done the same thing." He yelled "Don't you ever use that pot again. You have to use the doggone outhouse, you go out. Don't use that pot again." That boarder didn't say a word, he was embarrassed. It served him right for using my pot. I peed in his boot, that's what I did!

When we were all well and happy we would run around and get into some mischief. I came into the house flying and maybe hit a corner of the table or I'd bump and hit the chairs. I was always hitting the chair and it would flop over and mom would say "San Antonio, can't you walk into the house easy?" Mom would call me *Stombalone*.

And I remember the women used to go out and do their wash on Mondays and hang the clothes in the back yard. They would talk over the clothes line with the woman next door and they would say, "For the love of God!" When they would talk about the children, they would say "Jesus Mary and Joseph!", and always have some nice invocation. And that's how they would talk as they hung up their clothes.

Our parents always taught us when we came downstairs to say Good Morning. We would say "Buon Giarno". Sometimes us boys would come down and not say a word. On Sunday morning my dad used to be there. And he would say, "You come downstairs like a *chooch*. Only a donkey enters a room and doesn't say Good Morning!" So we learned to say Good Morning. (Donkey In italian is *asino*)

When we went to bed at night we said, Good Night. We said it in Italian. *"Bonna serra Ma, Bonna Serra Pop"*. He'd say *"Bonna Serra, Bonna Serra"*. We'd climb up the three floors. We go up to the third floor, jumped into our straw mattress and go to sleep.

Sunday afternoons were good times in Waynesburg. All the men would gather. One fellow used to come out and he had a guitar. My dad always used to have a guitar and the minute he would start playing the guitar, here comes another fellow from the hill his name was *Lugu*. He played the mandolin. Oh, he could play the mandolin swell. And then my brother Johnny would join in with his accordion. We had a boarder named Carmen, we used to call him Carmenella. He had a homemade whistle made out of a cane with holes through it. He sure could play that whistle.

They would tap their feet to keep time, and oh they made wonderful music. All the kids would gather around. We loved to hear them play. And of course some of the men and the women would start their little Italian folk dance, and they would go around in a circle. I remember this big Italian woman, Carlotta. You know, the big stout woman. She would get in there. By now they had drank one or two glasses of wine. They weren't drunk but they were feeling kind of happy. And they were dancing and oh, they had such wonderful times.

After that the men would start playing *Morra*. You know what *Morra* is, pronounced *Morda*. They throw their fingers and they call out numbers *Sette, sette, otto, otto, due, due, Morra!* (7, 7, 8, 8, 2, 2, Morra!) One hand keeps score with their fingers. If you throw down a finger, you guess what the other fellow's gonna throw, and you call a number. If the fingers match the number you call, that's a point for you. Oh they used to play that game six at a time. You'd hear *Sette, sette, otto, otto, morra!* That's the way we'd spend our Sundays.

I remember the time my future Aunt Jessie came over from Italy. My uncle Louie wanted to marry so in those days they took each other's pictures, and if you liked the pictures you'd say, "Yea, I kind of like that man or I like that woman". Like a mail order bride. Jessie came to live in our house until Uncle Louie set up a home and later they got married at the church in Morges.

And oh, could she sing. She was a beautiful young woman. She had blond hair and would sit there and she would sing. People would say "Sing us some new Italian songs." We were hungry for some good Italian music. She would sit there and sing Italian songs that she knew. I would sit around her and one song she sang I remember in particular. I still remember to this day. It goes something like this:

Bionde cubella bionde say come-ay-londa
My peach a sheen my peach akay.
Bionde cubella bionde say cumma londa.

And oh everybody would love that, and we would clap, "More! More!" She sang until she got tired. Then, one by one, people would drift back to their own homes and break it up. Those were some of the happy times.

(I never could figure out the actual song and lyrics that he was referring to here. I transcribed it as it sounded directly from the tapes. I know it has something to do with a blonde woman.)

All the boys from town didn't like us boys from the hill. They always used to pick on us. When we were goin' downtown, they used to say, "Get back on the hill you Hunkies, Dagos." They used to call us Wops, Spaghetti Eaters, all those kind of names. So every time we went to town, they would run us out.

One day they were in a gang, six or seven of 'em. This particular day those boys come up to the hill. They were much bigger than us. They thought they could push us over, you know. Like I said we had a lot of dogs, like my dog Topsy. One of these big boys, kind of a bully, started taunting us. They'd put a chip of wood on their shoulder and say "Try to knock it off, try to knock it off". They all did that back in those days, trying to start a fight, see.

And this one big boy was shovin' me around. Naturally my dog, Topsy, wasn't gonna stand for that. He came over there, and he started barkin' to defend me. Of course when one dog starts, all the other dogs come. Oh about ten or twelve dogs, boy they came over there, and they started growling. This boy lifted up a hand. The dogs would dash up there, and stop with their tails straight up in the air showing their teeth and growling. These boys would all back up you know. "You guys got those dogs" he said. "Come around here once without those dogs and we'll show ya." But they didn't bother us. Those dogs really protected us. Yes, those dogs were really something.

Now and then in the summer there was a boy, name of Ronnie. He was the meanest boy you could find. In fact when he went to school, the teacher brought him out to the hall for a paddling. He did something wrong, he always did something wrong. He took the paddle away from the teacher and he hit her across the legs and gave her a big black and blue mark. Then he threw the paddle down and ran out of school. Naturally he was expelled.

He was mean. He had a little brother who used to tag around him like a little dog. And that boy, he used to pick on anybody who was small. He used to beat 'em up, especially me. We used to have a little grocery store up on the hill. This one day my dad said, "Vic, go up to the railroad station and find out if any of our groceries came". We were expecting to get some groceries. So I went down there to check, and I waited. When the 6:00 train came, I waited while they unloaded all the passengers and freight and stuff from the baggage car. They were no groceries, so I started walkin' home. And here Ronnie comes from around the corner, and he gave me a slap across my right cheek. Oh, he almost knocked me over. Then that little kid said, "Hit him again Ronnie, hit him again Ronnie." I started to run, and he started to laugh, you know. He used to do that all the time.

Another time we were down at the brickyard where they made coals. There was nobody around but me and Herman. I don't know what we were down there for. And here the kid comes and he started pickin' on me. He punched me, and he knocked me out. I was knocked out, and his little brother was kicking me you know. Herman was afraid of him, he wasn't there defending me at all because he was afraid Ronnie would jump on him. Finally he had his fun. I lay on the ground, and I wouldn't get back up. He left us alone, and he went away.

About a year later, Herman and Gene and a bunch of other kids went down there swimming, and here was mean ol' Ronnie down by the brickyard walkin'. They said, "Hey, let's take that doggone Ronnie and throw him in the reservoir." There was a big reservoir near the brickyard on the side of a hill so the water would have pressure to run down. So they said, "Let's throw him in that big reservoir because he's always hittin' my brother and pickin' on little kids. So yea. Let's do that." So Herman and Gino said, "C'mon Ronnie, I'll show you a nice place to swim." So Ronnie went along. He was afraid to pick on anybody when more than one was there. He wouldn't pick on 'em. See, he was a coward. Only when you're alone, then he would jump you, he never would jump a gang.

So they took him up there, it was about thirty feet deep, a great, big, round reservoir. You know, there was a big pipe on the bottom where the water would rush down and go down to the brickyard for the boilers to make steam. They got him and they threw him in there. Then they ran to beat heck. But Ronnie could swim like a fish. He pulled himself up over the rails, climbed up and said, "Why'd you boys throw me in there for?" They said "You stop hittin' our brothers or we'll throw you in there again!" You know, I think after that he didn't touch me.

One day when Ronnie was walking through the hill he had a great big gash on his heel. My mother saw that it was all festered and full of pus. She felt sorry for him so she took some peroxide. I'll never forget, my mother took the peroxide and washed his wound and bandaged it. She told Ronnie "Keep it clean now or it will get infected". So he left us alone after that. He sure was the bully of the town.

In the year 1919, the Great War ended. We had just gotten news that the war was over. They dismissed school and we went out and rang the school bell. A bunch of us boys from the hill, we ran toward this big Methodist church that was close by. We pried open the window, crawled in and we rang the bell. All the church bells in town were ringing. We were so happy that the boys were gonna come home from the Great War.

When we got home to the hill we told our mothers who hadn't gotten the news. They had no radio back in those days. "The war is over! The war is over!" So we got a bunch of tin cans and sticks, and we were hittin' em, makin' a lot of noise. We all went down to the mine to wait for my dad and all the miners to come out of the mine. Oh, there was a bunch of us, boys and some girls along too. When the cars came out of the mine and my dad came out and saw us kids with drums beatin,' he said "What's goin' on out here? What are you celebratin?" We said "The war is over! The war is over!" Oh, they were so happy! You could hear the church bells ringin', and the shop started blowin' the whistle. We had two brickyards in Waynesburg, the Whitacre Greer & The National Fireproofing Co. They were both blowin' their whistles, you know, and the church bells were ringin'. Everyone went home and was so happy.

The next day there was a big celebration in town. They had these great big republic trucks and cars. And the people were on those trucks, and us kids jumped on too. We were so happy. They had streamers and everybody was makin' noise. The American flag was draped over the truck goin' up and down that Waynesburg Main Street. And they had a band, a little Waynesburg band. They started playing some of those war tunes. And here's one of the tunes that they played:

Over there, over there,
Send the word, send the word over there,
That the Yanks are coming,
The Yanks are coming,
The drums rum-tumming, Ev'rywhere. [10]

That's the kind of fun we were having, going up and down the street shouting, "The war's over! The war's over!" And we'd throw streamers out, and the whole population would come out. Everyone was so happy, waving American flags. All the school children, they would be parading, and oh, that was such a happy occasion that the war was over. The bells were still ringing, and the two brickyard whistles were still blowin'.

---

10   From the song Over There by George M. Cohan

Then the band would strike up again with other wartime melodies.

Yes, those were the days in 1919 when the armistice was signed. Of course then everybody broke up and went back home. Then about six months later the boys started coming home. Shiploads after shiploads of American soldiers came home. I remember the first soldiers that came back to Waynesburg, especially a guy from the hill. Here he came with his crutches. He was limping you know, he was wounded in the knee. And lots of our boys came home with one arm, a lot of 'em were in hospitals. It took a long time for those wounds to heal.

I remember going down to the post office to pick up our mail during the wintertime and seeing all those big posters on the wall with big, big cannons, red flash fires, soldiers lying on the ground, dead. And the big picture of Uncle Sam with his big American suit. And he says, his finger pointing at you, "Uncle Sam Wants You!"

And we used to buy Liberty Bonds to help finance the war. We used to buy them at school and, for twenty five cents you would get a stamp. When you get the book full, well then there would be a bond. They used to call them Liberty Bonds, and we did that in school to help the war effort.

Remember me tellin' you that we had a little horse? Well this horse now was nothing but a bag of bones. He was a swayback. In fact, when I rode him bareback my butt used to get so sore on that big back bone of his. There was nothing but ribs and bones. So his days were over. My dad wanted to buy a Model-T truck, he was talkin' about it. So well, we knew we were gonna have to get rid of the horse. We had to take him out in the woods, across the river, not too far.

So Herman and me went along with my dad to take the horse into the woods. I remember digging a hole big enough that we thought could bury the horse, see. We let the horse stand by the hole, right by the hole because he was heavy. So my dad told me, "You stand back there!" So Herman had to draw the rope. Of course the horse never moved he was so old, you know. His head was hangin' down, his ears flopped, you know. That horse, awwww, he was pitiful.

So my dad had borrowed a gun. We never had guns in the house, so he borrowed a gun. And he shot him right between the eyes. Boy, that horse dropped, and he fell in the hole alright but not all the way in. So we had to put him in the hole so we could bury him. So I remember me getting a hold of the hind legs, Herman got a hold of the front legs and my dad got in the middle. We just gave it a heave and the horse fell back and the four feet was up in the air.

Now he was an old horse and he was stiff. Anyhow, his four feet was sticking straight up like four fence posts. Oh, we couldn't budge him, and we couldn't get him outta the hole. My dad said, "Aww, let's bury him anyhow". So we buried him. We got done burying that horse, heh heh. All you could see was four legs stickin' up. Four legs and that's the way we buried that horse.

Now in later years when I was workin' in the Hercules factory in Canton, I used to tell about that old horse. The guys at the shop told jokes about it. They used to say that what we did was took a couple of planks and put them over the horse's legs to make a picnic table so we could go out there and have a picnic. Heh heh. That's the kind of jokes they used to crack about that old horse. Aww those were the days.

(I remember this particular story. I thought they really <u>did</u> put planks over those horse's legs and make it into a picnic table. I remember telling and retelling that story as a young girl….I didn't realize it had been embellished. I must have been naïve!)

Another thing we used to do in the summer when school was over was this: There was a barn there, a big barn. This barn wasn't like any other barn you see around, this barn used to hold seventy, eighty mules. The mules were used in the brickyard see, and they were kept in the barn. It wasn't very far from where we lived, just across the road there. We would go in the upstairs of the barn and play in the hay. There were a lot of big hay lofts there, it was pretty high. We would play hide and seek. Especially on rainy days it would be a good place to go play.

We'd spend all day there see. And we would go way up in those rafters. We would climb up the ladder all the way up to the roof. We could touch the top, see. At the spot where the post held up the room, the hay didn't go around the post tight. We would shimmy down those posts and that would be a good hiding place for us to stay. Oh we could've smothered in there, you know. One time three or four kids got in the same hole and we all told them, "Get outta here I can't get no air." And we would hide until somebody would find us. Then we would hop from place to place. And ohhh, we would have fun.

Outside of the barn there was a great big straw sack where they used to thrash in summertime. They'd get these great big thrash machines with great big cleat wheels. And boy when they blew their whistle and steam would come, you'd get so excited, you know. "Oh, they're gonna thrash, they're gonna thrash, let's go to the barn!" And we used to follow that big tractor, you know with that big combine on the back that does the thrashing of the wheat or the oats or whatever they're gonna thrash. And on the back would come a water wagon that would carry water for the steam engine. And it would fill it up. They would go to the barn and the engine would get to the one place with this big, long belt tied to the lead wagon. Finally it would get to the big hay wagon that was used to cover the oats to feed the horses with and the mules. We used to watch that machine thrashing away, awwww we used to watch it there all day.

Then there was a great, big straw stack. We used to go up on this stack, and we used to go right up on this stack and slide down. Boy was that fun. We used to have so much fun.

When we were kids on the hill, we had no mattress like you have now. Ours were made of straw. Mom made a great big bag, and we'd go to the barn and fill it with straw. And that straw would be our mattress. Naturally us kids would sometimes wet the bed. There were three or four of us, and it was always gettin' wet. Mom would turn the mattress over from time to time. When the straw used to get too bad, we would change it and get new straw. In the summertime it used to get kind of heated, and naturally it would form a lot of bedbugs. And that's how the hill got the name, heh heh bedbug row.

And of course my mother used kerosene on it once in awhile to get rid of 'em, or they would swarm all over you. You just brush em off you.

That's the kind of life I had when I was a kid.

Then when summertime came and school was out, there was a fellow who had four or five ponies. He also had a little mine, just a hole in the ground really, a small mine. I never worked in his mine, I worked in the big one. So one summer he asked us kids from the hill if we wanted to work hoeing corn for him for five cents a row. And these rows, my gosh, they went from one end of the field to the other, oh so long! We hoed and hoed. We'd get down to the end and then we had to come back again. Eight or ten kids would take ten or twelve rows and come straight down, see.

Naturally we got tired of it, and we got careless. We started choppin' the weeds, and we chopped a lot of corn. When we would chop off a corn we would stick it in the ground and plant it, you know and naturally the corn would never grow. Well that farmer didn't want to pay us. One Sunday a long time after the end of summer, that fellow came up the hill. The men always played cards, drank wine, played accordion and they always had a lot of fun up there on the hill outside dancing. They had a pretty good time you know.

So my dad said to him, "Hey what's a matter you? These boys worked for you hard and you didn't pay 'em for that doggone corn!" He asked us how many ears we picked. So we told him how many rows we had at five cents a row. It had to be forty, fifty, sixty cents. That was a lot of money. And the man said, "Hey those boys cut off a lot of corn. I went down there and a lot of corn was broken off and dried up. They chopped up too much corn. If they chopped only a few corn that wouldn't have been so bad. I ain't gonna pay for what they chopped". Naturally my dad had him cornered so he paid us, but he didn't give us as much as we wanted. Later he wanted us to do another whole field. We turned him down. Nothing doing. We're not going to hoe corn for nothing.

I'm gonna tell you a story. This story is about a bum by the name of Charlie. He used to sleep down at the brickyard. He would come up on the hill and beg for coffee. We gave him the old coffee grounds that had been boiled, and he took those grounds and reboiled them in a tomato can. He would boil himself coffee, potatoes, onions, eggs or anything he could get to eat along with some bread.

Charlie liked beer. So up on the hill everybody had empty cases of beer outside. They always drank a lot of beer. First we'd take a couple of empty bottles of beer. We would look good because sometimes there would be a little bit of beer in some of the bottles. So we'd pour it out into one bottle. We'd search all over the case and find another bottle maybe with half a bottle of beer left. A few drops, here and there and we'd make about a couple of bottles of beer. We put the tops on, take 'em down to the brickyard and give 'em to Charlie. Boy he used to like that. He used to look around you know, sit by that kiln on chilly days and wring his hands and make a funny noise that sounded like "Hah! Hah! Hah!" And we thought, "Why does he do that for?" It was just his habit, he'd be hunched back rubbing his hands.

One summer all of us kids said, "How about playing a trick on old Charlie?" We knew he liked beer. So we decided to have a little fun. A bunch of us boys went down to the brickyard, and we took an empty beer bottle. "Let's all pee in this beer bottle". So we all peed in the beer bottle, you know, heh heh. We got it nice and full, and put the top on it, tight. We shook it up and got foam on the top, you know, just like beer. The color of the pee was just like beer. We had to wait till the bottle got cold so it wouldn't be warm in his hands or he would suspect something. So we got it nice and cold, you know. We put it in the water for awhile and chilled it off.

Then we went down there, and there Charlie was. "Hey Charlie, want a bottle of beer?" He said, "Thank you boys." So we put it down, and we left. We all went and hid behind the tiles. First Charlie took his tomato can out, then he reached in a bucket and took a potato out and he put it in there. Then he boiled that. Then he reached in another bucket, pulled something else out, a piece of meat or anything that people gave him and put it in the same can, and made like a mulligan stew. It was a great big tomato can. He had this thing goin' you know. We waited and waited. "C'mon! Drink that beer!" We could hardly wait.

So he finally pulled the potato out and peeled it. He reached in his side pocket of his big, long coat. That coat was torn and patched, and he took out a long piece of paper. He put a little salt on the potato. Then he reached over into the other side pocket and took out another long piece of paper and put a little pepper on the potato. Then he reached in his knapsack, and he had a big, dirty hanky. He had bread in there. He took a hard hunk of bread and he broke it. He ate some of that bread, ate that potato. Finally he reached over, and he got that bottle of beer and he took a long drink. Whew! He spit it out. He threw it against the tiles, and broke it. He was mumbling, but I don't know what he was saying. Boy us kids took off. That was a dirty trick we played on poor old Charlie. But that's what we did.

In the wintertime we'd find things to do. There's a river that runs thru Waynesburg called the Big Sandy River. In the winter they would cut ice so everyone would have ice in the summer. We used to go down there and watch. The men would go down to the banks of the river with a team of horses pulling a big sled and wagon. The wagon would be low to the ground see, that's how they would get around in the wintertime. The men took a hatchet and cut a hole into the ice, and then they took a saw, a great big saw, and used it the same way you would cut wood. One guy would go down into the water and saw that ice into nice big blocks.

When he had big stacks of ice sawed, he would cut the other side of it into squares. Then he took ice tongs and grabbed these big hunks of ice and slide 'em across the ice. Two guys would take one block on each end, and load 'em into the sled that was covered in straw. So they'd take this here ice to this great big open shed. They would make a layer of sawdust on the floor first, and then put the ice on top. They kept a space between the ice, and then they put sawdust all around the blocks. Then they put sawdust on top, then more ice until it reached the top of the shed. The sawdust was good insulation so the ice wouldn't melt. That's how we got ice for our icebox. We had no Frigidaire's then, nothing but iceboxes. When summer came they took a big hunk of that ice and sold it. That's how we got our ice.

There was a pond, a great big pond you know. Us kids used to play hockey with a broomstick, a pick handle or anything we could find to use for a club. We'd take a piece of wood and carve it up, and that would be the puck that we would hit. Of course we had no skates, we couldn't afford skates. We skated with our shoes because our shoes were made of heavy leather on the bottom. Once you got 'em shiny well they would slip. We would fall on our butts many a time. But we would skate around there and hit that puck, you know. We would have a lot of fun.

Then we would go back behind the kilns there where they baked the bricks. It was nice and warm, and we' go back there and just warm ourselves up till we got good and tired. Then we'd take off and go on home. And that's the way we spent our winters doing things like that. And of course sleigh riding and going to school during the week days. I had happy boyhood days.

One Saturday I was walkin' down the dirt road, and here comes the beer wagon, with two big Clydesdale horses. I wanted to hitch a ride on the back. The horses were gallopin' along and I wanted to ride. I was small, you know, and I had to jump up and get a hold of the big end gate, that way I could ride. So I got a hold of the end gate with my hands, and I jumped up, and I hung on there. I would ride on this wagon hangin' onto it with my two hands. And that was a lot of fun. Just then the wagon went across a big bridge over a brook. Clank, clickety, clank, clickety, clank, across this here bridge. The empty boxes of beer were bouncing up above. When we crossed the bridge the wagon hit a big rut. The wheels hit that rut, and the boxes jumped up and they come right down on my finger. Boy they caught my big middle finger. Ohhh, I let loose and my finger was black and blue. Oh my God it hurt. I told my mother, I hurt my finger but I didn't tell her how. She put it in hot water, and well that finger got pretty sore. In a couple days the fingernail was getting loose. Every time I would pick something up that nail would come up and hang there like a hinge. I used to work it back and forth. The other kids used to say, "Ooh don't that hurt?" I would say "Well yea, but it's got to come out". It was too tight yet to pull it off, so one day I got tired of that and I gave it a tug. Out came the whole fingernail. So I lost my fingernail just takin' a ride on that big beer wagon.

Another time, me, Pete Romie, Ben and a bunch of other kids were walkin' on the railroad tracks when along comes a freight train. We always liked to ride the freight even though we were told not to. We were runnin' on the side of the box car you know. We'd step on that bottom rung of the step ladder, and we would ride on that train. When the train started to pick up speed, all the other kids jumped off. They hollered "Jump Vic, Jump! Jump!" But I was afraid because the ground was kind of hard there. I thought "Gee I'm gonna hurt myself." So I kept on a goin', ridin' that train till I came to an embankment where there were ashes that went all the way down the slope. I figured ashes would be soft so I thought, "Here's a good place to jump." So I got ready and I jumped. I rolled down that embankment like a rubber ball. I rolled and rolled right down to the bottom. I got bruises and scratches, you know, but that's it. The other kids came up, "Did you get hurt? Did you get hurt?" When they saw that I wasn't hurt they said, "Let's go swimming!" We weren't very far from our swimming hole. So we went down to the river to swim and wash some of the dirt off.

Another day we were going through the woods, we were always goin' into the woods. This time my brother, Herman, and a bunch of big boys and I went along. Herman said, "Vic you better not come along. We're gonna cross a river, and you'll be afraid to cross that bridge". It wasn't a swingin' bridge, but it's something like it. So I went along anyhow. Herman said "Ok, we'll leave you behind if you don't cross the bridge!" So we went through the woods lookin' for mushrooms. We were always lookin' for mushrooms, and we found em too.

We came to the Big Sandy. This was a different end of town from where we lived. It was what they called the dam. It was a small dam, and the water ran the Magnolia mill. Well, we got to the river and all that was there to cross over was two cables tied to a tree on both sides. There were boards nailed up the trunks of the trees that you could walk up like a stepladder. What you had to do was hold the top cable with your hands and walk on the bottom cable, see. So the big boys went across. They got a hold of the top wire and they edged themselves across.

Now when I got up there, well I couldn't reach the top wire because I was smaller than the other boys. You know, I couldn't reach it. I said, "Herman I can't reach the top wire". He said, "Well too bad, I told you not to come. You either got to hold yourself on the bottom wire or go back home." Well I didn't wanna go back home. So what I had to do was get a hold of the bottom wire, and hand over hand, I had to get myself across. So I tried it. I got about to the middle and ohhh my hands were getting tired. It felt like my arms were gonna break. The water was swift and deep, and I couldn't swim. So I put my arm up over the cable and hung on there with my elbow, see, to kind of give my hands a rest. That wire was rusty and little jaggers were on there, and it was scratching and pinching me. And oh my God I said, "What am I gonna do? Herman Herman I can't make it!" He said "C'mon a little bit more, you're halfway across. Make it, you can make it. C'mon." Well I tried it; hand over hand, slowly, slowly. Finally I got close to the shore, and I let loose and dropped down on the soft bank on the other side. Ohh, I rubbed my arms, and I took some water and washed them off where I pinched it with that wire, you know. And those were some of the things that I did during the summertime.

We always raised hogs. So Pat and I went back to the farms again to buy two little baby pigs. We would tug the sled behind us and come back home with two little baby pigs. We'd put 'em back in the shed that we had then we'd go to our barn to get a lot of straw for the pigs. Those little pigs would get under that straw and hide. When we'd go there to feed em, no pigs. "Where's the pigs?" All at once they would pop out, nice little pigs, two little white pigs. You know they'd dash out there to their trough. We'd put their feed there, and they would grunt you know and look at us with their big eyes.

In the winter time we had what we called butchering day. That would be the day we butchered our two hogs. Every year we would buy two little pigs, and we would raise 'em, see. Then in winter when they would be nice and big and fat, we would butcher the hogs so we would have meats and sausage and whatever else mom made.

So on a Saturday morning we got up early. We had a big, black three-legged kettle. We filled it full of water and boiled it. We had to get the water boiling because you need to take the hair off of the pig after you butcher it. A couple of men would help my father with butchering. So when the water was boiling we went into pen and let one hog out. We led him to the spot we wanted to butcher him, not very far. We didn't feed the hog the night before, so he would be nice and clean inside.

We just gave him a little bit of water and maybe some ground corn. Naturally the hog was kind of hungry. We would lead him with corn, and he would follow the corn to the spot where we wanted him.

We didn't have a gun in those days, we used a knife, a big long knife. So two men got a hold of the hog's ear and a couple guys got a hold of the hog's legs. Right away the hog would scream. You know, they squeal, I don't know why, but when you catch a hog, they squeal.

They picked up the front leg of the hog, right where his heart would be, and they'd stick this knife in that hog. My job was to hold the bucket to catch the blood, because we used the blood see. And I'll tell you later how we used it. The hog was a screamin' and squealin', and the men would use the big knife and poke in there all the way up to the hilt. Out would gush the blood in this bucket. Pretty soon the hog would just naturally, stop and die.

Then we'd take the blood and take it in the house. It was nice and warm. Mom would take a big handful of salt and put it in this bucket and put it on the stove to cook. When it was done she would dump it out, and it came out like a jelly mold. She'd make what they call blood pudding and blood sausage. Then we went outside to watch how they did the rest of the job.

The men took burlap sacks and put it over the hog. Then they would take the boiling water from the big kettle and pour it on top of the burlap sack the way you would dip a chicken into hot water to pull off the feathers. That way the hair would come out easy. They would take a scraper or knife or whatever they had, and scrape the side of the hog. It would end up nice and clean, just like it was shaved. Then they flipped the hog over and do the same thing to other side.

We had a three-legged tri pole that we used to hang up the hog afterwards. Next they slit the hog's hind leg and use that muscle there to hang him up on this tripod. They would cut him in half and take all the insides out, the liver, the kidneys, the heart, we used everything, you see. Even the lungs and the spleen we would eat. The tripe, we would pickle that and we would have pickled tripe and pickled pig feet. Oh we used everything.

Then we cut the hog all the way down and left the snout hanging together so the two ends wouldn't flop over and hit the end of the tripod, and we'd let it freeze overnight. The next morning we'd take the hog down and cut it up. My mother would take the hind legs and the front legs and cure it to make bacon and ham. All the meat was cut it into little squares.

We had a big meat grinder. We'd grind all the pork and make our sausage out of that. Then she'd make some blood sausage. She'd take some of the meat and some of the blood that we cooked and she'd grind it all together. It would be kinda red. We'd have blood sausage and your regular sausage. And plenty of garlic in it! Aww that was good. We hung it up in canes up in the attic to cure it. Then all the bones and stuff, we used to cure 'em with pepper and salt in big boxes and put these up in the attic to cure. Then we would have these bones to put into your sauce or to make a big kettle of soup beans.

Now when we were butchering this hog, an American guy was passing by there delivering some milk. He said, "Hey you guys, you know it's against the law to make a poor animal suffer? Now why do you use a knife? Why don't you shoot the poor hog, it's quicker. That way he doesn't have to suffer." So when it was time to butcher the second hog he said, "Well let's get a gun and do it." So they did. It wasn't my dad that shot him, he was no good with guns. So this guy shot the hog in the head three times. He wouldn't fall. He was just squealin' and makin' noise. My gosh it was tough. So here comes another guy who said, "Here use my gun!" Man he pulled out a gun that looked like a cannon, a big revolver. Bang! One big shot and boy that hog just fell right down. Real quick.

We picked him up and took the knife between his front legs. I held the bucket again, and we did the same thing again. That's how we would have our meats and goodies, always with plenty of garlic. That's why I love garlic. Garlic may have kept everybody away, but we never got sick, eatin' all that garlic.

Now for the last time I'll tell you a few more stories of my boyhood days in Waynesburg. One summer day I was babysitting my baby sister, Jenny. My mother had to go to help some neighbors who were sick. She was gonna go for half a day, and I was stuck with the baby. Jenny at the time was just a little baby. So here come all my friends, Pete, Romie and all the rest. "Vic Lets go to the barn and play". I said, "Oh, I can't go to the barn today, I have to babysit my sister." They said "Oh cmon, we'll have a lot of fun, take her along." I said "Gee that's an idea, maybe I will. Mom won't be back for a long time, maybe I can beat her back home." So I did. I, heh heh, I did.

I took little Jenny, I always put her across my hip; you know and carried her In the back of the house, up over the road to the barn. Oh the kids right away started climbin' up those ladders to the hayloft. So I put Jenny down right on the barn floor. I sat her right down in the middle of the barn floor with hay on either side of her and on the back. It was a big barn made like a "T". Oh, a huge barn, about 80, 90 mules were kept in there you know, so it had to be a pretty big barn.

We had a lot of fun in there. So after I put her down I climbed up the ladder. We used to go way up on the rafters all the way up to the ceiling. Then we'd jump down on the hay mound. Oh we had fun. We didn't pay any attention to the time. And then John, the barn boss who takes care of the mules, went in the pasture to open up the gate to let the mules back in. See, he had all these mules out in the pasture, he let 'em all out in the morning.

John opened this big gate so the mules would come in. They were supposed to go down up under to where the mules stay, down under the barn, you know. But when they came close to the barn they saw the big barn door was open and they knew that's where the hay was. Well they all walked in this here barn, oh about ten of 'em. They came right into the barn and was eating hay on the side. "Vic Vic" Pete said, "The mules are down there with your little baby sister!" Oh Jenny was cryin', she was a' cryin'. "Oh my God, they're gonna trample that poor kid to death!"

Well I scrambled down those ladders you know and I went between those mules. I was afraid, but I had to save my little baby sister. So I went down there and finally shooed some mules on the side. You know they have a habit of kickin', and that's what I was afraid they were goin' to do. So I grabbed my little baby sister, Jenny and put her on my hip and boy I scrambled up that ladder. And I held her there. Then John saw the mules weren't comin'. "C'mon get outta there you mules, get outta there!" He had kind of a whip, you know. He snapped the whip. Then they all left, and I came down. So I said, "Well, I think that's about enough for today." Jenny was still cryin' you know.

So I started to go back home. Now when I got home, mom was already there. She said, "Where'd you take that child?" Right away Jenny said to Mom, "Ma, Baca mange me!" Mom said, "What'd you say honey?" In Italian she said, "Baca mange me!' Which means in English, "The cow was gonna eat me up!" She called the mules cows, heh heh heh. She said, "Baca mange me!" Heh, it was kind of cute, but mom didn't think so. She said, "You mean to tell me you took this poor child to the barn? *Cio che lei ci do, uesto povero lei ci sono bambini muoiono e ottenere calpestatida parte della muli?* That means: *"What you gonna do, you gonna have this poor child die? And get trampled by the mules?"* Well I caught heck, I didn't get a lickin' for it, but I caught a good scoldin'.

About a week later, I had to babysit again. Down below our home was the railroad tracks and beyond that was a big corn field and then the Big Sandy. You could see it from the hill way off in the distance. We could hear all the kids down there playin'. There was a place down there where we would hunt for crabs. We would throw over a stone, see a crab, and then grab it. There was a bunch of kids down there and they were having fun. I said to myself, "Gee those kids are havin' a lot of fun. I'm gonna go down there too."

So boy I took Jenny across my hip, heh heh, and I ran down the railroad track, across the corn field and down to the river. I sat her down on the bank, and told her "Don't Move!" I got into the water. It was only up to your ankles there, it wasn't very deep. I started turning over stones catching those crabs, having fun, splashing around. And just then I heard my mother calling from way up over the hill "VITOOOOORIO! VITOOOOR." One boy said, "That's your mother callin." Ohhh, I grabbed my little sister, Jenny put her across my hip, ran across that cornfield and up the railroad track and home.

Mom was waiting. *"Che cosa voletge fare, volete uesto povero bambino annegare?"* She said, *"What do you want to do, you wanna drown this poor child?"* *"Si vuole annegae il suo?"* That means, *"You wanna drown her?"* And, heh heh, I caught heck. Good thing my dad wasn't home. But that's the last time that I ever attempted to take Jenny out.

It seemed that all the boys on the hill, one by one, were starting to move away. So our gang was starting to get smaller now. We went to the barn this one day, Herman, myself, Pete, Ben and a bunch of other ones hunting for rabbits. Now Herman had a 22 rifle. It was a Remington, a nice rifle. It fired a single shot at a time. Back in those days it wasn't a repeater.

So there was a big hay wagon with the bed of it lying down on the ground in the weeds. The men would haul in hay, and then they'd take the wagon off and lay it down on the ground, see. There was a rabbit under there, and we were trying to get that rabbit. Pete Vinci put in his hand and couldn't get him. Herman said, "Now keep your hand out from under there. You all get back boys, and I'm gonna get down there and I'm gonna shoot it." So Herman got down on his belly, and he looked under the wagon where the rabbit was.

Well Pete Vinci was so anxious to get the rabbit; he stuck his hand in there and tried to grab the rabbit at the same time Herman fired. Pete got the rabbit all right, but that bullet went right through the rabbit and got him right in the arm. He was shot in between the elbow and the wrist. "Oww!" he jumped up and said, "What'd you do? I've been shot!" I said, "He told you to keep your hand out of there, what'd you put your arm in there for?" Pete said, "I know it's my fault. I know what you said." Anyway we had lots of witnesses there that he was told not to put his arm there but he did anyway, tryin' to grab the rabbit.

Well that scared us you know, and we felt sorry for the boy. So we went home, and he must not have told his mother because nothing was said. But then the next day his mother came over to the house. He had gotten an infection during the night. He went to old Dr. McCormick and here he pulled out that little bullet, that little 22 bullet that was in his arm. He pulled it out and Pete told the story. His mom got mad. "Your boy shot my boy in the arm, and I want you to pay all the doctor bills." Herman said "It was his fault, he got in the way. We told him to not put his arm in there." It soon died down, and nothing was said about it. The arm healed up in a couple weeks and he was soon as good as new.

I want to tell you about another little incident that happened to me one summer. One night there was a movie show in town in the old city hall, kind of a good show. A bunch of us kids from the hill, we all went to the show together this certain night. They had a curfew there, see. We weren't allowed out in the street after 7:00PM, and the show started about 7:30PM just after it got dark.

So a bunch of us kids went through town and there was the town Marshall. He said, "What are you boys doin' here? You know you're not allowed out in the street after 7:00PM." Well we said, "We're goin' to the show." 'It's too early for the show," he said, "Go on home, you have time to come back." So we went in back of the alley. Heck we didn't want to go back home, so we circled around the alley. We stalled a little bit and took a different road. We finally went to the city hall and bought our tickets for a dime. The show only cost a dime.

It was an old William S. Hart picture. When the show was over, instead of goin' through town the way we usually do, some of the bigger boys said, "Hey let's take a short cut. Let's go through the cemetery." We smaller boys were afraid to go through the cemetery at night. I went through it in daytime many a times, but not at night because everybody was afraid of the cemetery because of ghosts and things like that. We were afraid of it. So these big boys said "Let's go!"

So us smaller boys naturally, we just followed. We went down the road to the left that led down to the cemetery. There was an iron gate in the front, and we opened the gate and walked in. We were about halfway through when one of the big boys said, "Look over there. Hey, Right there!" We looked, but it was dark, and we could just see the shadow of the tombstone. Right there was a big, black shadow, of a man. He had a big, long black coat, kind of a slouch hat, and he stood up straight, leaned over and put his two hands on the tombstone. He leaned over toward the path where we were and said "Why don't you boys shut up and let a man get his sleep. Can't a man have any peace?"

And oh we just got scared when we heard that and we ran. We heard kind of a cackle laugh. Of course he scared us. We didn't know what it was. The bigger boys knew what it was, but we didn't. So the next day we said, "Hey was that a real ghost we saw last night?" One of the big boys said, "No, that's an old bum that always comes through Waynesburg to find a place to sleep. Everyplace he goes; they always kick him out, or put him in jail so he decided to go sleep in the graveyard where nobody would bother him. He goes in the cemetery and lies in the nice soft grass on top of the tombstones. He used the tombstone for a headpiece. He put his coat there, you know. When we went through there we were disturbing him, so he thought he'd give us a scare. And boy the rest of my life I never went through that cemetery again.

Now talking about cemeteries and ghosts, a story comes to mind I always used to repeat to my children and I didn't tell it to my grandchildren yet, but you're gonna hear it now for the first time. It's about a woman with a golden arm. There was a rich man and he had a beautiful wife. Oh, she was beautiful. One day she got into an accident, and she lost her arm. Well he didn't want his pretty wife to go all through life with no arm, you know. So he decided he'd have an artificial arm built for her. But he had it made out of gold. He was rich, and he could afford it. So he made her a beautiful golden arm. You could move the fingers and all.

When she dressed up and put a glove over that hand, you couldn't tell she didn't have a natural arm. And everybody in town knew she had a golden arm, but you couldn't tell by lookin' at it because she had it covered. A couple of years later the woman got sick and she died. Her husband buried her, the golden arm and all. And now some of the big boys said "That arm is worth a lot of money. Why don't we go to the cemetery and dig her out, and take that arm. We'll melt it down and sell the gold and get a lot of money out of it. Yea that's a good idea."

So one dark night, three or four of these big boys, went down to the cemetery. Nobody around, not a sound, you know, everybody was asleep. They dug her out, took the box, opened it, took her arm, put her back and covered her up real nice so nobody knew the difference. They took this arm and started to go out of the cemetery. Then they heard a voice behind them saying "I want my golden arm." They got scared. Oh they ran out of that cemetery as fast as they could run, through the gate. There was a big tree on the other side of the gate. They hid behind the trunk of this big tree.

And the voice was right behind them, "I want my golden arm." Oh now they were frightened. They took off. Oh, they ran so fast. They came around the corner of their house and hid but the voice was right there close "I want my golden arm." Now they were petrified. They opened the door, ran into the house and hid under the staircase. They heard the voice almost on their neck "I want my golden arm!"

Terrified, they ran upstairs and hid under the bed. They were shakin' and shiverin' you know. Oh, they were really afraid. Then they heard the door open and they heard footsteps, clump, clump, clump, clump, clump, comin' toward the bed. Oh my God, she's gonna get us now. "I want my…" BOOM!

Now that was supposed to scare you out of your boots. If I didn't scare you, I didn't tell the story right. That's the story of the lady with the golden arm.

Here's another story: It was a hot day in August, oh it was hot, you know, I really was sweatin'. So a bunch of boys said, "Let's go swimming!" So we all went down towards the brickyard, down around the railroad tracks and around the bend to our swimming hole. All we wore back in those days was just a shirt and a pair of pants held up with little suspenders. And underwear, Heck this hot day we didn't put' em on cuz we knew we were gonna go swimming and the less clothes on the better.

So heck, before we reached the river we had our shirt out and all we had to do was just drop our pants and jump in the water. And when we get close to the swimming pool we shouted "The last one in is a monkey!" So we all scrambled down to the little slope that leads down to the swimming pool. Everybody jumped out of their pants, threw their clothes into a pile and then we would jump in, you know. Oh we would splash and swim, and oh, we would have a good time.

Some of the bigger boys would jump from the diving board. Now some of the bigger boys played a dirty trick on us. They would sneak out of the water first and take our shirts and pants and tie big knots right into the arms of our shirts and into the legs of our pants. When it was time to get out of the water and get dressed up, us little kids, me, Ben, Pete, and some of the smaller boys would find our clothes all tied into a knot. And we could hardly get the knots out.

The big boys headed home, and here we were stuck down there. Pete and I were the last ones there, and we finally got the knots out so we put on our shirt. Up the railroad tracks we went. And ohhh we were trying to take the knots off of our pants. Ohh we worked and worked, and we couldn't get 'em off. So I said, "Let's sit down and see if we can help each other." So I remember sittin' down on that railroad track, and that track was so hot we burned our little butts. Ohhhh. Man we jumped up and heh heh, rubbed ourself "Gee that's hot!" So Pete and I we tugged and tugged and we finally got' em loose. We put on our pants and tried to catch up with the other boys. That was a dirty trick that they used to do, tie our clothes into knots.

Then later on we did the same thing to some of the smaller kids. Of course we used to stop and help them. They couldn't get their knots out, so we'd stop and give 'em a hand. But the other boys they didn't help me and Pete. Boy we'd have to get 'em out ourselves.

I wanna tell you about another adventure that we had one summer, us boys from the hill. This time we had quite a gang, About 10 or 15 of us, maybe more. Herman was along this time and Pete, myself, Ben, Romey and quite a few boys from the hill, even Clyde Mann. He's the one who lived in our old house before they moved down closer to town. Well he was up on the hill that day and we told him we were goin' thru the woods for a hike and he said, "I think I'll go too." This was the first time he ever came with us. I'll never forget, but he came along this particular time. So we went down past where the barns were. We didn't stop at the barn this particular day.

We were headed for the woods to hike through the meadows to see what we could find, you know, chestnuts, or things like that. So we went down and we were talkin' with the smaller boys following behind. We came to a big black barn. We called it the Black Barn because ever since it was built they never gave it a coat of paint. That barn was just black, you know. So it got its name the Black Barn.

Now beyond this black barn was a great big pasture. It was several miles away from home. We went across this big meadow and came to a fence on the other side. There were, oh I would say about ten or fifteen horses that were in a great, big pasture with a big fence a couple miles long. I said, "Hey I've got an idea. Let's catch one of those horses and ride one." Yea, everybody thought that would be fun. So, we said "I'm gonna get' em." So the horses saw us comin' close and boy they took off with their tails in the air and their manes waving in the wind. They just took off like lightning to the lower end of the pasture and outdistanced us. Then they came to the corner almost where the fence was, and they kind of stopped and bowed and were eatin' grass.

So we came closer to 'em, and they were stampin' around you know and not moving. "Hey, let's form a long line and hold hands!" I remember we each held out our arms as far as our arms could stretch. Each boy would hold the other boys hand and we made a big long line. We kept goin' towards these horses to try to keep 'em all bunched up. We got pretty close to 'em and some of the big horses looked kind of wild to me. They kind of reared their head up and were plowing the earth with their front hoof you know, whining, stompin' the ground and runnin' around in a circle.

Some of the small kids got scared and broke the line and ran towards the fence. A lot of the horses ran out except three. We had three of 'em cornered there. So we formed the line again, and we came to the corner, "Ho there, ho there, ho there!" we kept saying "Ho, nice horsey, nice horsey." We kept comin' closer. "Don't move fast boys, move kind of slow so you won't scare them. I think we're gonna catch one." So we got close to one horse and we tapped it. That horse stayed, lifted up his head and we got him by the mane and held him.

The other two horses saw their chance and they dashed out, but we had this one. The other boys came close and we tapped it and petted him. The horse got used to us and he calmed down. We wondered, how are we gonna ride him? We don't have a bridle. So Pete said, "Hey we got some strings in our pocket, let's make a bridle from the strings!" So we took that string and put it around the horse's nose so we could guide him. We put it around his nose twice and up over his ears and tied it around his neck and made two little strings on the side. We asked "Who's gonna ride him first?"

Clyde said, "Let me ride him, let me ride him first." We asked "Why should you ride him first? This is the first time you came along with us and you want to have the first chance?"' He said "Yea, I have a pony so I got experience. I know how to ride the horse. You guys don't know how to ride. Let me break him in first. Then you could ride him after." So we let him ride. We put Clyde on and got out of the way. One of the kids gave the horse a slap on the rump, and that horse, he took off. And boy he ran across that meadow and man was he a-goin'!

There was a little brook, and anytime there was a stump or a brook, the horse had a habit of jumpin' over it. Well this horse took a big leap and jumped over the brook. The string broke and down came Clyde. He fell off that horse, and the horse just took off to join the other horses. Clyde was cryin' on the ground. When we got to him, his arm was completely twisted. He broke his shoulder. Ohh, he was cryin'. He was in pain, you know. We went up to him, and we felt sorry for him. We picked him up, you know.

"Oh my God", we said, "This is terrible. We should never have ridden that horse." Well Clyde asked to ride first. We couldn't catch that horse, he took off too fast. But who slapped him? So we took Clyde home, and he was cryin' the whole way, his arm was just twisted. When his mother saw us comin' she said, "What did you do?" He said "I fell off a horse. We went out in the woods and we caught one of the horses that belonged to Whitacre Greer." His mother turned to us and said "Why'd you put him on a horse?" She blamed us for getting her boy's arm broken. She called Dr. McCormick and Clyde ended up with a broken collarbone and bruises. His arm was in a sling for a long time.

There was another boy that we knew named Frankie Orlando. He lived about four or five homes below us. One day we were just lying around the house when we heard a scream from a woman. She screamed and hollered and was cryin', a hysterical cry. Everybody started runnin' down to that house, the women with their aprons on to see what was the matter. When I got there, the house was full of grown ups and I couldn't get in. "Whatsa matter? Whatsa matter?" And they brought the mother out. She was a cryin' and she said *"Povero figlio, Povero figlio ha perso la suo mano."* That means, *"Poor son, poor son, He lost his hand."*

Here's what happened: His father worked in the mine like my dad did. That was way before I started workin' in the mine. I was a child yet, about ten years old, maybe not that old. Frankie took these little mine caps. Do you know what a mine cap is? It's a dynamite cap. It looks like a shell that is half empty. They would put a fuse in this cap and then pinch the top. And then they twist it into the dynamite, see. And when that there cap goes off, it sets off the dynamite and that's how they blow up that there coal. The farmers used them too to blow up stuck trees. That little cap has got fifty pounds of pressure. See it's pretty strong.

Anyway, Frankie would take these caps home and put a short fuse on it. He would go down to the river and throw 'em in the river, and that concussion would kill the fish. And then they all come up to the top dead, see. He had a long pole with a net and he would get into the water and fill up his net and get a whole bucket full of fish. He didn't do it too often. There were guys watching and when they heard shots going off, reported him. Anyhow he got caught by the fish warden and paid a big fine for it.

That's what this boy did. He found one of those caps that his father had in the house, and he was playin' with it. He finally took a match to it, and the thing exploded with a terrific BANG! His mother heard the terrible explosion and heard little Frankie cryin'. Oh that was a sight. His mother was tellin' the women later on that the shell tore his hand into shreds. It was just hangin' there, completely mangled.

The neighbors took her out and sat her down saying *"Porta fia, porta fia, porta fia de mama"*. It means *"Poor, poor mothers son"*. It was a shame for a young boy like that to lose a hand. When Pete Vinci came down there, he saw the commotion. He said to me, "Vic, whatsa matter, whatsa matter?" I said "Awwwww, Pete, Frankie Orlando lost his hand". Pete was confused. "Lost his hand? How'd he do it?" I told him, "Awww with a dynamite cap." And so we all stayed there.

Now my dad never took caps like that home. He never kept guns and stuff at the house either because he knew heh heh, that I would have gotten into it or some of us would have gotten hurt. And I probably would have. You know a boy is curious and we hear a cap explodes and we think that is fun. But we don't realize the danger in those caps. So that's how the poor boy lost his hand.

When they took him out of the house I saw his hand wrapped in a towel completely covered in blood. And Dr. McCormick had made arrangements to take him to a Canton hospital. When he came back home about two weeks later, his arm was all bandaged up. Here he was minus a hand. They had to trim it up in back of the wrist. And he had no hand at all. And his father said, "I blame myself. If I didn't have those mine caps at home my son wouldn't have lost his hand".

Now about a year ago I was at the mall at Belden Village. I met my brother, Herman, there and we were talking. And here comes this fellow. He said, "Hello Herman I haven't seen you for a long time." I didn't know who the fellow was, see. So we were talking and Herman said, "Here's my brother, Vic." The fellow said, "Oh yea, I haven't seen you for a while too. You don't remember me do you?" I said "No I don't." Well Herman said, "You know him. He used to live in Waynesburg. He used to play with us all the time. This is Frankie." I was shocked. "Frankie! How are you? Oh my God." Then I shook hands with him. Here I noticed his sleeve was open and no hand. Oh I said, "I sure do remember you." Then we just talked. I didn't wanna bring up about his hand, you know, we just talked.

The 5th grade was the last year I went to school. That next fall I did not return to school. Instead I went to work in the mine. I was a Trapper. The job consists of turning switches, opening mine doors and doing chores like that. That job is called a trapper, that's why they always called me Trapper. Well anyhow I was too young, and the school board went to my dad and told him that I was too young to quit school. Even then I could only have a job with permission from my dad, that's the only way I could quit school. So I had to return back to school.

So I left the mine and had to go back to school. Going back to school was an embarrassment. When I got there class was already in session. I rapped on the door and the teacher answered "I am expecting you. Are you Victor?" "Yes I am." "I'm Mrs. Rushworm, your teacher. Welcome to my class, I'm glad to have you. Class, this is Victor. I'm sure you all know him. That's your seat back there, go and take your seat, the third seat from the rear."

Anyway I sat back there. I used to love to tell stories, I always telling stories. We had language class that consists of papers with a picture. This particular day the picture had three doors. You had to make up a story of what was behind those three doors in your own words. So my story was that behind the first door was a lion, the second door a bunch of bees, dangerous bees and the third door was a princess. I made up an interesting story of how I found out which door the princess was behind.

One key would open up any door, of the three doors. Open the wrong door and the bees would sting you, and you would die from poisoning. You open the lion door, and you would be killed. So you take the key and open the right door and there would be the princess. Then of course you would marry the princess and get half of the kingdom and live happily ever after.

By spreading honey on one door, I could hear the swarm of the bees. I don't remember what I used to find what was behind the door where the lion was. Anyhow the teacher said "What an interesting story." I worked it up to a climax you know.

One day we were talking about mining. The question came up, Why is there rats in the mine? How did they get there? Why do they go into the mine? The teacher said "Victor you worked in the mine, can you explain that?"

So I explained. "Rats are not in the mine, they are brought into the mines. Then they live there and they multiply so there's always rats there. There's reason to keep 'em there. The reason is if there is any danger in the mine, like a cave-in or gas the rats will give it away. They will start going out of the mine or they will change locations. The rats would get away from where they were and go someplace else. That would be a warning to the men.

In some of the big mines they used canaries in cages. If a canary would die, they know there's gas in there. The canary would die first and that would be a warning. Well that's why the rats are in the mine. They're in there to be a warning in case of danger.

They are fed whenever the mine is not working. There's a lot of grain put there special for 'em so they won't leave the mine. Otherwise they would get hungry and leave the mine. So that's why rats are in the mine." And the class thought it was interesting. They used to enjoy my stories. They would say, "Vic makes up some of the finest stories!" That's what I did.

I think I'll close up for now with my theme song. In the meantime I'll say to you children be good boys, mind your parents and I'll say goodbye, so long, and may God bless you, until we meet again, goodbye for now.

Chapter 5:

Working Days

My father taught me to work; he did not teach me to love it.
Abraham Lincoln [11]

After I completed the 6th grade I was allowed to quit school and go to work in the mine. Now I'll tell you some of the experiences that I had on my first job working in the mine as a Trapper.

My job was to take care of three air doors; you know, open and shut the air going from the right entry to the back entry to make a complete circle so everybody would get air into the mine. There was a big fan on the outside pumping the air in. Then when the motor men would come with 21 empty cars, the trick was to put the motor straight, going fast, turn the switch real quick and let the cars go on the side track. And that way the motor men could tip the 21 cars and head out. Then each driver would come and say I want so many cars. I would cut the cars and each driver would take their cars and go.

In the meantime we used to sleep under the big bench they had there under the rib. The rib was kind of a pillar. One day we heard the motor men coming so we all got up. We got our mules and got our stuff ready for another trip. All at once, down came the roof, the coal, everything and smashed that bench we were lying under to smithereens. Had we not moved from under there, I wouldn't be here telling you the story now.

So we had to empty all that stuff into the empty car, and send it out so we could build a new bench and start over again. We didn't consider the dangers of the job. It was dangerous, but we just loved to work in the mine so much that we didn't look at that part.

A few years before I started to work there a few men were killed

---

11   Abraham Lincoln

near where my dad worked. A man was setting charges of dynamite, and somehow one of the fuses got wet. He went back and relit that fuse, but he never got away. The thing exploded and killed 'em all, three men killed there under that load of coal and clay. Since then that place was always haunted.

Those guys would roam there, see. Many men saw a man with a long coat and a pick over his shoulder. He would be carrying one of those old lamps they had in those days with a wick, like a kerosene lamp before the car lamps came out. That was before my time. Anyhow, this one Monday morning, the driver he was sick from drinking too much over Saturday and Sunday. He said "Hey Trapper, Would you go back there and get the car?"

So I took this mule, Jenny, and I went back there and picked up this car, you know. I was heading back when all at once the mule started to walk on the side of the track. I said "Get in the middle there!" If the mule didn't move back he would pull the car off the track. And then that mule's ears popped up. He had seen a ghost which I didn't see. Right away I knew what the mule was seeing and I got scared.

I stayed on that car you know, and he pulled the car completely off the track. He shook that doggone car so much that the coal was leveled off and scattered all over. And that mule, I couldn't get him stopped. I hung onto that car for dear life until we came to a switch and the car just hit the switch and got back on the track itself. When I pulled into the place the man there said "What's a matter?" I told him "Oh, the doggone mule got scared, he seen something there." And then the foreman said "You mean to tell me you sent the kid back there? Don't you ever send him back there again. Now you know doggone well that place there is haunted. The kid isn't supposed to know about it, now he knows about it and he'll be scared." I wasn't scared, but I never went back there again though, I'll tell you that.

Another time you know I was supposed to go up one side of the mine to the other. It was called the right and the left. I was going to the right and I took a short cut to the old workout places. There were swamps in there, water and stuff you know. Well my car light went out, and I had no matches. I was left completely in the dark. I thought to myself, "Oh my God, how in the heck am I gonna get out of here?"

Now I remembered what my father had once told me, "If you ever get caught in the mine, just follow the track out." So I put my hand on the track and started going, going until I hit a dead end. "Uh oh," I said, "Well I must be going the wrong way." So I reversed myself, and went the other way. As I came around a bend I saw a light way off in the distance. There were big lights up above, and I saw that light so I got out. I went back to work and never told anybody that I got lost. That was really an experience.

One particular day the foreman of the mine said "'Trapper I want you to come to work early tomorrow morning. We're gonna clean some of the track in the mine." Once a week different fellas would clean the track. All the clay and coal falls on the side of the tracks and it accumulates and eventually covers up the tracks. So from time to time the tracks need cleaned off, see.

So I went to the mine that particular morning. When I got there he said "Trapper, I don't have any picks or shovels here. How about you going in the mine and borrow two picks and two shovels from one of those rooms where the men are working." That would be way in the very end of the mine. The mine was about two miles long, maybe longer. It was quite an old mine, you know – big. So I hated to say no to him, because of the experience I had before with that mule. Remember the mule saw the ghost, and the car got off the track. The mine was haunted, and I was afraid of that. But I was ashamed to tell him.

So I started going into the mine all by myself. I walked and finally came to this spot where the mule got scared. Boy when I came to that spot I just ran, man didn't I run. I ran so doggone fast. I got past that place, took two shovels and two picks from the first room that I got to and started to come back. Oh no, I had to pass the same spot again. I was afraid of that.

So I was walking along, and whether or not it was my imagination or me thinking about it, I looked to one side and saw a light in the distance coming toward me, kind of flickering. I looked at that, and just stood still. Oh the sweat was rolling down my back, and I just froze there. I just kept lookin' at that light and imagined I heard swishing of water, somebody walking in mud. You know how a boot would sink into mud and make a squish, squish, squish, squish sound? "Oh my gosh, what is that?" I said to myself, "Aw, maybe it's a lot of rats walking along there. It could be that."

So I started taking small steps, I couldn't run. I just kept walkin', walkin'. Oh my gosh. The light kept coming, but it never reached me. Just then I heard a rumbling noise and there was the foreman. He was coming in with the motor to get me. Why he didn't take me in with the motor at first, I can't understand. But I imagine the reason for that was they don't turn the power on till a certain time and I had headed into the mine before that time. The foreman saw me, stopped and said "Get in."

So I got onto the motor, put the picks and shovels on it and we started on the way out again. We came to spot where we had to clean and we took our shovels out and cleaned the tracks. We got in a day's work, and went home. That was the end of that experience. It sure was a scary one for me.

Another day my dad got hurt. We had a phone in the mine, and I used to answer the phone. This particular day I got a telephone call. A man said "Hey kid, bring the stretcher up here. Somebody got killed up here." So I took the stretcher and I ran up there. I said "Who was it?" The man looked at me and said "No, he didn't get killed, but he's badly hurt. Kid, it's your father."

Ohhh my God, I tell you I just went back to my place, took my bucket and I started going out of the mine. When I got home, they had already put him in an ambulance and sent him to Canton. He had a broken pelvis, broken ribs, broken shoulder, cuts and bruises all over.

Had Herman been with him at the time, he would have gotten killed. Herman was working with my dad and had gone over to get a bucket of water. My dad was loading the clay and the whole load of coal on top hit the car and broke. Good thing it was wet because it broke up and buried him completely under it. When Herman got up there he just saw my dad's hand sticking up. He scratched and got him out Oh I wanna tell you, he was a mess.

The night before this happened my mother had a dream about my father's mother, my grandmother. So In the dream my dad's mother told my mom, "Don't let my son go to work today because he's gonna get hurt. Keep him home, don't let him go to work. Don't worry but he's gonna come home covered in blood with his clothes torn and coal dust all over him. I want you to take the white basin and towel and wash him up, clean him up."

The next morning when my mother woke up she said to my dad, "I had a dream about your mother. I wish you wouldn't go to work." Herman and I were standing there with our big buckets packed, a big trio of buckets. We packed a big meal. In those days I used to eat quite a bit. My father said, "You old women, always thinkin' about dreams, I don't believe in that." Mom said "No, I wish you wouldn't go, I'm afraid something is going to happen today." Pop said "Awww, C'mon boys lets go. Women are always worrying about something."

So we walked down to the mine. We always rode in those little cars, you know, with the mule. There would be so many men in each car, about four or five mules and we would go in and each man would go to their particular place to do their work. A little later I got the phone call.

They loaded my dad up and took him straight to our house and then called Dr. McCormick. The doctor came and said, "Get him washed up, and I'll call Canton. We'll get an ambulance and take him to the hospital."

So my mother took the big white basin and a big towel and she washed my dad's face. She washed all the black coal dust from him and all the blood. There was a big gash on top of his eye, and cuts and bruises all over his eye. She cleaned him up and put a clean shirt on him. He was sent to Canton just the way she dreamt it would happen. It's strange you know that my dad didn't believe in dreams then a thing like that happens.

I want to tell you about one more dream that my mother had. Shortly after my dad died at the age of 89 she had a dream. She dreamt that my dad said "Sabett, Sabett." Sabett is short for Elizabeth. In English you say Lizzie instead of saying Elizabetta. In Italian you would say Sabett. He said, "Sabett, go in the clothes closet." We had a clothes closet where we kept all of the slippers. She had some kind of a bag where she had shoes and slippers. "In there you'll find a $20 bill stuck in the toe of my slipper. I want you to have it." So my mother she woke up. She was thinking about this dream all day, of how it seemed so real. But she was doubtful.

When me and my brothers came back from work that night she said, "Boys, I had this dream." After she told us about it, she went and got that slipper just the way he described it. She got that slipper and went down into the toe, and wouldn't you know she pulled a crumpled $20 bill out that was in the toe of that slipper where he had kept it see. She opened it up and here it was a $20 bill. And you say you don't believe in dreams.

So now came the time we were going to leave Waynesburg. After my dad got hurt in the mine, he couldn't work anymore. So my mother decided that we should move to Canton. Oh I hated to leave my beloved Waynesburg. I loved those hills. No more goin' through the hills and swimming. In the last year I was just startin' to swim a little bit, I got more courage. Then we moved from Waynesburg and that was the end of that. But anyhow we had to leave see, and I had a sad heart.

We left and we moved away. We had Topsy the dog. We took him along, but mom didn't want to. So we lived in Canton about a week. Our dog naturally wanted to make friends. He wandered along the alleys there trying to make friends with the other dogs. Mom worried, "I don't know, we're not supposed to have dogs in the city. Nobody has a dog. I don't think we can keep the dog." She said, "Get the truck, Herman and Vic and take him to Waynesburg." So we took poor Topsy in the truck and we went toward Waynesburg. My Uncle Louie and Aunt Jessie lived up in the hill there about four or five houses from where we used to live. Topsy knew them since we went there quite a bit. So the dog went to live with Uncle Louie.

I remember the winters we had here in Canton. It wasn't like Waynesburg. We used to go to town often. We used to call it window shoppin', that's what we did. Herman, Pat, me, and Ben used to walk uptown then go back home and Mom was getting ready for Christmas. Dad would buy the fish. He'd buy the squids, eels, smelts and bacala and she would prepare 'em. We used to decorate the house. We would put streamers from one corner of the room to the other and a wreath in the window. We would put a kind of a big bell that you open up like a fan that you hang up in the center. And that's the way we enjoyed our Christmas. Then we'd go to midnight mass.

But before we'd go to church we used to play bingo on the table. We'd play for pennies or nickels. Then we had another game that we played called *Sarientaful*. We put a big pile of cornmeal on the table and we would play. We would put five pennies in there or a nickel and mix it all up in the cornmeal. Then we divided it into piles of how many players that there was. Then we would dig thru the pile to see what we got. Some would find ten cents, fifteen cents, some would two pennies and some would find nothing. And that's how we would play that game. After that we would take off and go to midnight mass. It always was crowded at St. Anthony's Church, you know. We were all single, and we used to walk to church.

The day came when we finally bought a model-T truck. That was a joy. Boy to see a 4-cylinder truck you know that was really a joy. Herman used to be the driver and later on Pat. I wanted to drive but my dad thought I was a little too wild to drive so he didn't let me drive. So one day Herman said, "Go ahead and drive, but keep it down at the garage". We didn't have a garage at the house so we kept it at the dealership garage which was a little distance from our house. So me and Ben went down there to pick it up, but it had a flat tire.

"Gee the tire's flat. I'll put some air in it." So I got an air hose there to put some air in it. Ben said, "That's enough, that's enough air in there, Vic, that's enough." I said "Ohh a little bit more, a little bit more". I kept putting air in, then BOOM the tire exploded. It tore a big gash in it you know. "Uh oh. Oh my God what am I gonna tell my father now?" I got home and I told him what happened. Oh he got mad. Dad said, "Don't you ever touch that truck again." And you know he never let me drive after that because I broke that tire.

I just realized that in all of these stories I mention all of my brothers, but I never mentioned my brother Johnny. He was just a small boy when we moved to Canton. He was a happy-go-lucky kid you know, full of pep. I remember he used to have a little wagon. We used to go down to the city dump that was on Cleveland Avenue, which is now Route 77. We used to go there in the morning and wait for the trucks to come. They used to throw away crates. In those days crates were made outta wood. Johnny used to break 'em up, put 'em on his wagon and tie 'em up. Then he'd come home with a great big load of kindling wood and put it in the garage. That's what my dad would use to start the coal furnace. This was before we got a gas furnace.

So day after day Johnny went down there, and he'd spend all day there. One day he came home and my dad said, "Where you been? You've been gone all day, you're always out." Johnny said, "Oh that's what I get, I stay there all day, wait on the trucks to come to bring home all this kindling wood, then I catch heck. So I ain't gonna go down there no more and get the wood." Naturally our kindling pile started to get low. So my dad said "Hey we need some more firewood." So Johnny said, "Well every time I go down and get it I catch heck." My father did appreciate that Johnny went down to get the kindling wood for the stove, so Johnny started going back. But he did stay all day. He was a character.

Johnny was the one who gave Herman his nickname of Jake. I don't know how he started it, but he started callin' him Jake. "Hey Jake." And you know that name stuck with Herman for a long time. Even though we don't call him Jake anymore, sometimes Ben's wife, Vernie, still refers to Herman as Jake. So Johnny's the one who gave him the name of Jake.

Now Johnny lives in California. And I haven't seen him for quite a while. He really was something. He can talk a leg off of you. He's interesting you know, he can really tell you stories heh, heh. I thought I would mention Johnny because he's the only one of my brothers and sisters that I didn't mention in any of my stories so I didn't want to forget my brother, Johnny. That's all I'll say about Johnny.

In Canton when summertime came we used to go all over. We had that Waynesburg spirit you know, going through the woods. So we would take off. We had 3 cars (streetcars) goin' down in front of Market Street. Back in those days there were streetcars, clink clangin' down there. We never rode the cars, we always walked. We walked from one end of town to the other. We went all over Canton and into some of the woods that were on the outskirts. We went through all those woods, up McKinley Monument, up the steps and we had a wonderful time.

And as we grew up one by one, we got married. Herman he got married first, then my sister, Mary. Then finally I met a wonderful woman, Josephine. I used to call her Josie. We married and I raised a wonderful family of 5 children. I'll talk about that next.

I remember the times when we had our Christmas under the Christmas tree. Oh the joy to see my children open up their Christmas toys. And that's about all to say right now cuz too much to say. The tape is winding down. I'll talk about it on the next tape. I'll see you again someday. Well now I'll say goodbye and I'll put on my theme song that I always use.

Chapter 6:

Courtship

The greatest legacy a man can leave in the world is not so much a great business, but a "living" investment in the future, through loving, stable, employable and healthy children.
     Ian Grant, FATHERS WHO DARE TO WIN (1999) [12]

I got a job first at the Pennsylvania Roundhouse, but I didn't stay there long. I didn't like the work inside. Then I went to Timken's, and I worked there for five years. Then I hurt my back, and they wouldn't give me a transfer. I had back trouble for a long time after that. Finally I went to Hercules and I stayed there for over 43 years. While working there I got married and raised my family.

I had my ups and downs there, hard luck, hard work. I earned 35 cents an hour, 10 hours a day from 6:30 to 5 at night. That was where I was working when I met a wonderful woman.

Josephine Vitale was introduced to me by Philip and Pauline DeMario and we got engaged and soon we were married. Going back to the days when I was courtin' mom, I used to call her Josie. Later on when everybody called her Jo, then I started callin' her Jo, but I used to call her Josie. And she kinda liked that. Every time I'd go see her, she'd have cookies, you know, she'd have a big dish of cookies, see. And she'd have chocolate cookies on one side of the dish and another kind on the other. And she said, "What kind of cookies do you like?" "Oh I just love chocolate cookies, you know I love all kinds of cookies but I just love chocolate cookies."

So she passed the cookie sheet you know and I'd take a cookie. She'd say "Here, take more!" So I'd go to get a different kind and she'd turn her dish around, "No, no take the chocolate, take the chocolate." She'd keep turning the chocolate around for me. All the kids knew that I liked chocolate, so no one would take the chocolate cookies. They saved them all for me. Heck, I wanted some of the other cookies, I was

---

12   Ian Grant, FATHERS WHO DARE TO WIN (1999)

getting' tired of chocolate all the time. I didn't say anything to her, didn't want to hurt her feelings. She was having such pleasure giving me something that I really liked, you know. So every time I'd go there I'd always get the chocolate cookies. I didn't stand a chance; she always turned the dish to give me the chocolate....

(So that's how my dad grew to absolutely hate all things chocolate. He must have finally confessed it to her. But as far back as I can remember he never ate anything chocolate: cake, ice cream, cookies, nothing!)

On one particular day we were talking about gnocchi. I said, "My mom, she makes gnocchi" Jo said, "Oh, my mom makes 'em too." I said, "She doesn't make 'em often. But once in a while she makes a big batch. I just love 'em." So she said on another occasion, "I was telling mom that you like gnocchi, and she wants you to come over one night next week to have gnocchi for supper." I was excited, "Ok! Oh, that would be swell." I was kind of ashamed and timid you know, I always was. Her dad, he always liked me, and always wanted to see that I got plenty to eat. He always thought I was bashful and ashamed.

So supper was ready, and there was a great, big bowl of gnocchi there. Now what I didn't know, we make our gnocchi with potatoes, and they didn't. They make theirs plain. So naturally they're heavy and solid. Ours are soft and they melt in your mouth, really delicious you know. I didn't stop to ask, how did you make 'em. I just took for granted we all make 'em the same.

So here they heaped my dish, ohh a great big dish, you know, gnocchi all over, good gravy on it, you know. We always called the sauce gravy. All right. We sit down, all the kids all around the table. We say grace. I put one in my mouth. Uh oh. I knew they were wrong. I didn't like those kind of gnocchi.

Mom makes 'em this way once in a while, but she makes 'em different. She makes 'em with greens you know. And she makes 'em small, and she calls 'em *chicatell*. She didn't call 'em gnocchi, she calls 'em a different name when they're made without potatoes. These here were shaped like ours, shaped the same, but no potatoes in 'em.

And awww I ate that dish, and I ate that dish. I was glad when I finally got to the last one. I forced 'em down. I wanna tell you, I could bust. And my stomach felt like lead. No, I don't want no more! I took my dish and lifted it over my shoulder. Her dad said, "Don't be ashamed! When you come here to eat, you eat! When we got work, you work! C'mon!" He said, "This is no place to be ashamed." He took my dish and boy did he load it up, heaping full. "Mange, mange." That means, "Eat, eat". Oh gosh. I took my fork and I was digging around, and I put it in my mouth, and I'd eat. And good thing the sauce was good tasting. I tried to get as much sauce as I could. And I ate and I ate and I finally ate the whole dish. I ate two whole dishes of it. Oh man! I loosened my belt. My stomach was bulging. I felt like a rock. I was really stuffed to my throat.

I never told mom until way after we got married. "No, we don't make 'em that way. We make 'em with potatoes." Jo said, "Why didn't you tell me! Gee I didn't know." "Don't tell your mother, she'll feel bad." Even after we got married, I didn't want to tell her. So she said, "I have to learn to make 'em your way." And mom, she learned to make 'em the way we do with potatoes. And from then on we always had 'em with potatoes. And that's the end of that particular story.

(The famous gnocchi story never fails to bring a smile to my lips as I picture my polite father forcing down two heaping plates of gnocchi. As a child, I used to help my parents make gnocchi often. It seems we used to make them every few months.

They had a white porcelain table down the basement that was used just for this purpose. My dad would sit and run the freshly peeled and boiled potatoes through the potato ricer. He would make a great big mound. To that he would add flour, eggs and salt. He and my mother would form smaller mounds. Then my mother would take these and work them down into long ropes and she would cut each one, flip it with her thumb, dip it in flour and voila! We had gnocchi.

They had a homemade ping pong table down in the basement that was lined with sheets of wax paper. Each of the individual gnocchi were lined up on this wax paper like little soldiers, each one perfectly uniform in size. You'd better believe they formed perfect lines. My job was to count them. I always had the same job.

Then on Sunday all my brothers, my sister and all the kids would come over for a gnocchi dinner. Of course the sauce was homemade and delicious. What a treat!) See recipe on page 152

We used to go to the show you know. I used to take Jo to the movie show once in a while. Back in those days we had to take her little brother, Tony, along like a chaperone. Later on we used to go by ourselves.

We set the date to get married. We headed to the old Stark Dry Goods which is now the O'Neil's store in downtown Canton. We went down in the basement there where we could buy cheap curtains, something for the windows. So Jo put her purse down.

What I'm getting to see is one time I lost a dollar. Jo said "Gee you lost a dollar, here let me carry your money." So from that day on she always carried my money in her pocketbook. The day we went shopping for the curtains was payday. I got paid $50 that day. Now $50 was a lot of money back in those days. So she put the $50 in her purse and she carried it for me so I wouldn't have to carry it. I didn't have a pocket. She said "Gee you lost a dollar, lucky you didn't lose it all." So I gave the money to her, and she put it in her purse.

So she put the purse down on the counter and said to me, "Hold the end of this curtain Vic." She looked at the material then said, "Yea, I think this will do. I can cut it in half and make a curtain for the little window up in the attic. So we bought it, got on the elevator and headed up to the second floor. Then she noticed she didn't have her purse. "Oh gee I left my purse." So we rushed downstairs and looked for her purse, but it was gone. So we asked the girl if she found a purse, but no, no purse was there. She told us she would call us if it showed up. It never did you know.

We even put an ad in the paper that we would give a reward if we would get the purse back because it had some papers that she wanted in there and a check that she had made for her father for a certain insurance. That was gone too. You know we never did get that check back, never got that pocketbook back. Never. We lost that $50. And she felt so sick, so bad. I had to take my mother down there to calm her down.

"Jo don't take it so bad." I told her, "What the heck, $50, I'll make it again." And oh she was crying. "Yea" but if only I hadn't taken that money. You only lost a dollar; I lost the whole fifty dollars." I told her, "No, we both forgot to pick up the purse." That's what happened that day.

(See how kind my father was? How many of us are that kind and caring? In a similar situation would we be quick to yell and cast blame or like my father be just as quick and willing to soothe an injured spirit and take half the blame? We can all take a lesson from this.)

Chapter 7:

Family

A father is a guy who has snapshots in his wallet where his money used to be.

Author Unknown [13]

We set up a home at 114 Gerber Place SW in Canton. Our first born son came along, Jimmy. Oh we were proud! Such a fine baby boy he was. We let his hair grow long, nice and curly. 2 years later, yeah, my first four kids are 2 years apart. Then Leo, he was born, another fine boy. We always wanted a girl, but we were happy we got a boy. We had 2 fine boys. We used to go out shopping for the Christmas tree, you know put up the Christmas tree and the way they opened up their toys, it was a joy.

Then along come Patty. Small little girl, proud to have our first little girl, so small she fit into a little shoe box. Oh, we would dress her up in a nice little bonnet. She looked so cute, like a little baby doll. Then along came Victor. We named him after me, Victor Junior. But we never called him Junior because we didn't want to call him Junior; we wanted to call him Vic. Then after a space of about 9 years along came Maryanne. That wound up our family. She was a joy to have because in time everybody got married and we had her at the house.

Things went along pretty nice for our family. We always had enough to eat. We didn't have the best of food, but we didn't starve. Especially at Christmas or Easter, the kids can still remember how we used to buy a live turkey or a live chicken. I'd wring their necks and they used to watch me kill the chickens down in the cellar. I told them to hold the legs. The minute the chicken would start kicking, they would let it go and the chicken would bounce all over the cellar. We'd have wonderful dinners.

I used to take the kids to the woods and McKinley Monument. I tried to show them a nice little summer vacation, take them out

---

13   Author Unknown

different places. We used to go to the Cleveland ball games; we'd eat lunch by the lake there. And that's the way it went. Then of course in later years when my time came close to retirement, and I finally retired and my childrens were all married except Maryanne. She was the only one here at home. When she got married, I started traveling. I traveled all over. Mom, she came with me to Arizona, Colorado, New England, Blackwater Falls, and we even drove to Montreal, Quebec. We had a happy life, happy childrens and everything. Thank God.

I want to talk more about my five children for a little bit now if I may. Yep, Five wonderful childrens. How proud mom and I were of you boys and still are. Oh you brought joy to our lives; you've been such wonderful childrens. We sure are proud of you. We'll start with Jimmy first. Now Jimmy, when you were small, you got kind of sick. Oh you were getting pale you know, and so finally we called the doctor. I'll never forget it was Dr. Graham. And he looked at you and said, "Oh he's just got a little weakness in his chest, you know just a little cold". He gave him a little medication.

But Jimmy, you weren't getting any better. You was just sittin' there on the porch with no strength to play. This boy was sick! Everybody was saying, "This boy is sick. Why don't you try Dr. Fisher, he's supposed to be a good baby doctor." So we did. I went to work that day and during the day mom called Dr. Fisher. He came down to the house and he looked at Jimmy and said, "Oh my God, this boy has pneumonia. He has had it for awhile. I have to put him in the hospital." He was running a temperature. Oh, mom cried.

I came home from work, and you were lying in the front room on the sofa. We lived down on Gerber Place at the time. I came home, put my bucket down, and you were lying there on the sofa. I asked "Did the doctor come?" Mom said, "Yes, Jimmy has pneumonia. He has to go to the hospital!" And oh, I started cryin'. I went on my knees, put my arms around Jimmy, my face against his and I just sobbed. Oh my God.

So we made arrangements to take you to the hospital. It was called Little Flower, which was in town. It was a branch of Mercy Hospital which was then in downtown Canton. So we took you there, and you always wanted to sleep with a pillow. You always hugged a pillow. So we took you there, and the nurse said, "No, you can't have his pillow here, because we have our own and they've got to be sterilized." We told her

"He's gotta have a pillow or he won't go to sleep." So they gave him a little pillow, and boy he hugged that pillow. Every time he went to bed he had to have a small pillow, and he always hugged that pillow.

So anyhow they took care of Jimmy you know, and they drained his lungs. They said, "Boy, if we don't get his lungs clear, we're gonna have to tap him on the side of the ribs." Thank God they didn't have to do it. And the nurse used to take Jimmy with his nice, big, long, curly hair by the hand from room to room and show him the different kids. Well, when he got better, we brought him back home. Oh the nights we spent crying over that, hoping he would get better.

The doctor said, "When he gets better, we'll wait a couple of months and he should have his tonsils out because he has extra large tonsils and he can get a cold and get infected. I think we should take 'em out." So we decided to do it. So after Jimmy got well and strong, seven or eight months later, back to the hospital he goes to take out his tonsils. The doctor said, 'It will just be overnight, he'll just sleep there one night so he doesn't bleed. You can take him home in the morning."

So we took Jimmy again to the hospital. I remember he was in the room with other little kids. He had his little pillow along. They took his tonsils out, and everything came out fine. Finally we took him home.

I'll never forget, we had him in the living room. We took the baby crib downstairs so mom could watch him. "Jimmy, we have some ice cream for you." We always gave the kids ice cream when we took out their tonsils. Well that night we had spaghettis. Jimmy said "Oh, I want spaghetti, I want spaghetti." We said "Jimmy, you can't eat spaghettis. You got a sore throat, it will burn you." He started crying you know. I said "Jo, let's give him a little bit, he's gonna hurt his throat by crying too much." So we gave him some spaghetti. And, oh we were afraid that he might throw up. But we gave it to him. And, oh he ate all those spaghettis and drank Coca Cola® on top of it. And it never bothered you! You went through that like a champion. You were walkin' around your crib you know, you were rarin' to go.

One day we were in the kitchen and you were playin'. You leaned over your crib and fell out of that crib right on your head. Boom! We heard a noise and we ran in there, and there you were. You never cried. You picked yourself up, and we examined you. You ran all over the place you know. From then on we kept you out of the crib. You grew strong.

One night about a year later you got up in the middle of the night with a terrible earache. Oh, your ear was hurting you, and you came to our bed. "Mom, mom my ear hurts!" You were sobbing, and we picked you up. We put you in the middle of our bed and put our arms around you. We took your little head with the sore ear on the pillow. "Press on the pillow, Jimmy." We put our hand on your head to make a little pressure, and that eased the pain, and you closed your eyes. Everything would be ok now, you were safe. You were in bed with your mommy, and she would take care of you. And you fell asleep. That's the way I remember some of the hardships that we went through at the time.

Another thing happened to you too, about a year later. You got a big swelling under your jaw. It started swelling as big as a pear. My gosh we didn't know what that was. We took you to the doctor, and he said, "Oh my God, he's got a big tooth growing there. Instead of the roots growing up the roots are growing down towards his jaw. We're gonna have to stop that or we'll have to pull the whole tooth out." So they had to lance under his jaw to leave that infection out, the pus and matter. He still has a scar under his jaw. So look real close and you still might find a wee, little scar where he has been cut there. And you know that tooth stopped growing down and it grew straight. From then on Jimmy didn't have anymore trouble with his jaw.

Alright, now we come to my son, Leo. Well Leo, you were a nice, little, bouncing baby boy. But one ear, I think it was your left ear, it was kind of lopped over. And we didn't want you to go through life with a lopped ear. Then when you got to be a nice, fine young man your ear would be flopped over and guys would make fun of you. So we said, "We have to do something about Leo's ear." So we went to a plastic surgeon, and he said, "Yes, we can cut this and bring it close to his head and you'll never know it has been cut."

So we made arrangements and took you to the hospital to have plastic surgery done. They cut your ear and fixed it. Oh they did a good job. You can't tell where they operated on you. When you came home, I'll never forget, you had a big turban around your head. You looked like a sheik, one of those Arabian sheiks. And you wore that around your head for a long time.

And of course Leo, you had your tonsils taken out too. We thought we should have your tonsils out before they got bad. We said "Now Leo, you're gonna go to the hospital, we'll give you some ice cream." And you were happy; you knew that you were getting some ice cream when you came back. So when you came back home, everything was well and good. Your tonsils were getting along fine. You had all the ice cream you wanted to eat. And that's the way it went with you, Leo.

And now Vic, we had your tonsils taken out too. And you got your ice cream, and you came home from the hospital. Oh, mom worried about you childrens, you know, and cried over you, took care of you and nursed you.

So, we bought you a bicycle. We said, "Now Victor, be careful. Don't go too fast. You might get hurt." I think you were about 10 or 12 years old. So one day you came home, you had fallen off your bicycle. You hit the handlebars of your bicycle and chipped all your front teeth. And oh, you came home, and your front teeth were chipped and bleedin'. Boy there were sharp. You were biting your tongue and hurting your mouth. Well, I had to take you to Dr. Cain. And he said, "Well, I can't take him in, I'm all full." I said, "This is an emergency! He fell, and broke his teeth, and he can't work his mouth." So he said, "Alright, wash him up here."

I'll never forget taking you up there to Cain & Cain Dentists. He ground your teeth down and took all the sharp edges off. He said, "Well he's a little too young now to put a plate in. We'll just have to wait till he's a little older then we'll cap 'em." Well the way it happened was we never did do anything with your teeth. When you went into the service, you had that whole job done then. You finally got all your teeth back. So that's the way it went with you boys. So now I'll play a song for you boys....

(Here dad plays a rambunctious polka tune...)

Now I want to talk about my two little girls. Patty was my first born girl. When Patty was born, they had impetigo going around the hospital at that time. Impetigo is a skin disease, and when we brought her home from the hospital, just a tiny, cute little baby, her skin was covered with impetigo. Later on it changed into eczema. And oh, she had eczema all over her hair, head and body. She used to itch and scratch. Oh, in the night mom would stay up and put new bandages on you and tie your hands down so you wouldn't scratch your face. Oh, how we cried. We took you to Cleveland, to Pittsburgh, we doctored, did everything possible you know. You went though that. Later on when you got older, you did clear up, but you always had a little bit of asthma. And then the time came when we had to take out your tonsils too. And we had to take you to the hospital. And the same thing happened; we promised you ice cream when you came home. And you took it pretty good. Oh the pains and sorrows and hardships we went through raising you kids when you were sick.

Now Maryanne. When you were born, how happy we were that Patty would have a little baby sister. When we went to Dr. Agnone, mom was sick. She wasn't feeling good. And he said, "You're pregnant!" And we were surprised you know, because mom thought she was sick. Oh, how happy we were when you were born. And we took you home. Oh, what a sweet child. All the rest of the kids were already grown up, and you were small running around the house you know. We would dress you real beautiful like, you know.

You had your tonsils out too and got your ice cream. Then when you were a little older, you were complaining about pains in your side, always used to get pains on your side. So we decided to take you to Dr. Pagano. We told him "She's got pains on her side." And he checked you over. He pressed, and oh, it hurt. He said, "Yes, she's got a large appendix and needs surgery. I don't advise you to wait too long. You'd better get it done quick because it's liable to burst."

So, oh we took you to the hospital, and we had that appendix taken out. In about a week or so you came back home well and good. And then you got infection. Oh, you got a bad infection. You were running a temperature, and we were worried. And mom cried, and we thought maybe the operation went bad. And Dr. Pagano looked at you and said, "My God she's running a high temperature. What did she do? Did she eat something she wasn't supposed to?" Well the only thing we knew that you ate was some potato chips and some pop. We didn't know if that caused it or not. But anyhow, boy they put you in the hospital and worked on you and worked on you. Well they got the infection down, and pretty soon you was well enough to come back home.

(I was ten when this happened. I actually turned eleven in the hospital. The operation went smoothly as dad said. But then about

three days after I came home from the hospital, I had terrible pain. I couldn't walk without completely doubling over. My aunt Jenny drove me with my mom to the doctor's office. From there we went directly to the hospital. I remember my mom's voice breaking when she told my aunt to drive directly there. I was in the hospital for a week. During that time I received one IV after another. They would alternate one arm to the other. At one point, they put them in my feet. To this day they have a difficult time starting an IV on me. Anyway, I was almost completely out of it, I was so sick. My mom would come up to the hospital and sit by my bed all day long. After the fourth long day, my fever broke. The morning of the fifth day, I was feeling much better. I was allowed to sit in a chair. I wanted to surprise my mom. I heard her footsteps coming up the hallway. Her face looked drawn and sad. But when she spotted me sitting in the chair looking more alive then she'd seen me look in days, the joy on her face that I remember to this day brings tears to my eyes even now...)

I'll never forget when you got older, one day you went to play with a friend of yours from school. Her mother was a nurse. You fell and broke your collarbone. And oh when we went to pick you up, we knew there was something broken. We had to take you to the hospital. So at the hospital I'll never forget Dr. Pagano saying, "Hello my little girl you're back again. What's wrong now?" He checked you over and said, "Well mom don't worry. She's young, and she'll mend quick. She's got a broken collarbone." They had a collar around your neck to keep your shoulder still and not moving. And after a while, well you healed, got to be good and strong as ever and went back to school.

(I was 13 when this happened while playing a game of 'statue'. Remember that game? One person grabs your arm and spins you. However you land, you stop, like a statue. Well, I landed on my left shoulder. I actually heard it break and knew immediately something was wrong. I sat on the ground, feeling dizzy. When my friend, Bonnie, came to grab my hand, I shook my head no, saying I didn't feel good. They went on with the game, and I went into the house. I knew her mom was a nurse. I told her what happened, and she took one look, had me sit down, and immediately called my parents. I remember putting my head back on the couch and fading away for a couple of minutes. After my parents arrived, they took me to the hospital. Dr. Pagano set the bone with a quick jerk,

sizzling pain and it was done.

The padded brace fit around my shoulders and under my armpits. I remember having to stay in the house and in bed for almost a week! Seems crazy now. My mom put me in her bed and slept with me at night, while my dad slept on the couch. This was during the summertime, August I think. After a week, I was so happy to get out of the house and take a walk. I remember marveling at the smell of the fresh air, the sound of the birds, the color of the sky, the trees.

I was particularly upset about this event because I had been practicing to try out for eighth-grade cheerleading. With this broken collarbone, I couldn't put my arm up in the air to do my cheers and my jumps! This was a big deal to me. I continued to practice anyway, one-armed. When school began again, I refused to wear the sling, against doctor's orders. You could see the bump of the brace, but I kept quiet about it. I didn't want any attention. I wasn't due to get my brace off until two weeks after cheerleading tryouts. The day of the tryouts, I tried out with the brace on and did everything to the best of my ability. It must not have been good enough, because I didn't make it. I was devastated. In hindsight, had I let the judges know about my condition, it might have worked in my favor. But that never even crossed my mind. I made up for it the next year when as a freshman in high school I made the cheerleading squad.)

And then that was the end of your trouble as a child.

But you kids have brought lots of happiness and joy to us and I'll stop now and I'll play you a little song for you two girls. Now listen...

> *"You're the end of the rainbow, my pot of gold, you're daddy's little girl, to have and to hold, a precious gem......"(end of tape)* [14]

Children, this is your grandfather trying to tell you a few ways he tried to enjoy his boyhood days. God bless you all and keep you. I hope you have as wonderful a boyhood as I did only, in your way not in my

---

14 From the song Daddy's Little Girl, Written by Theodore Morse and Edward Madden

way. My way is kind of rough by today's standards. I thank you all for being such wonderful, wonderful children. And you, my wife, Josephine, for giving me five wonderful childrens and a happy life. And Maryanne, you were the joy of our life because you were the last one. When your mom was sick or we thought she was sick, and the doctor said "Oh, you're pregnant!" she said "WHAT!" At the time we were shocked, we didn't think that she was pregnant. But thank God, it was the best thing in our lives that you came along and made us very, very happy. You rounded out our family. I want you to know that I love each and every one of you very much. Bye for now.

Chapter 8:

Down Memory Lane

A man's children and his garden both reflect the amount of weeding done during the growing season.
        Author Unknown [15]

Good morning, this is the end of February, February 28th. Tomorrow is the first of March. It's a beautiful sunshine day this morning, beautiful. So Pat and I went to church this morning, and we went out to breakfast. I said to Pat, "Oh, it's a beautiful morning, what do you say we go for a ride." Pat agreed, 'Where do you want to go?' I suggested, "Let's go down to Morges. I'd like to see some of the old countryside from when I was a boy." Remember I was telling you about those back country roads, picking those berries you know.

So we took off. It was beautiful, takin' our time, ridin' around. And we went down to Waynesburg, up over the hill to the old schoolhouse, and we came to Morges. We parked the car, and took a walk though the cemetery. Aww, the names I saw on there, some of the boys I played with that are buried there. We ran across the grave, remember I told you about little Bruno, the little boy who had consumption? Well we ran across his grave. "Aww here's where little Bruno's buried."

Now as a boy, we didn't go to the cemetery because we had no way of going. I never saw his grave before, but now that I'm talkin' about those Waynesburg days, he comes to my mind. There he was, the tombstone, the letters almost faded you know, just could make out his name. Little Bruno, his picture was on there.

And we came across the grave of another boy that we know, his name was Gino Corsi. I never talked about him so much. He lived down toward the brickyard. We used to go down to his place and buy rabbits. Well, Gino was only 17 years old when he died. The way that he died was really sad. He was workin' down at the brickyard, pushin' these little cars with an electric crane. There's three wires that runs the

---

15 Author Unknown

electric. Put three cars in there and run the crane like you would run a streetcar, you know. Well one time the boys were foolin' around there and they got a hold of one wire. And see if you get a hold of one electric wire it doesn't hurt. But if you grab two of them it makes a complete circuit. One is a dead wire and one is a live wire. There are two outside wires that are dead wires, and the one in the middle is a live electric wire.

Somebody got a hold of two wires but they got the two outside wires, and Gino didn't know any better. He said, "I can do that." The other boys said, "Aww you're chicken." So he went ahead and grabbed the middle wire along with the outside wire. Well naturally he made a contact, and he was electrocuted. And the poor boy died, electrocuted. We felt sad and blamed the bigger boys for daring him. Anyway, we found his grave there, Gino Corsi.

Then, lookin' thru the cemetery, I ran across the grave of my Godparent, the one who baptized me. He also baptized Herman, Pat and Mary. He was Godfather to all of us. Dominic Mazocca was his name. Then we ran across his tombstone. "Aw here's my Godfather." I just couldn't remember him as a boy. I remember when he died. I went over to see him in his home lying in the coffin, you know. He had appendicitis. In those days they didn't know what appendicitis was. It burst, and before they could get him to Canton he died.

Walkin' around there we found old Father Mandray's grave. That's the priest that married my Aunt Jessie and my Uncle Louie. I remember us going to Morges in an old Touring car for the wedding. It was raining that morning, and she got married there. He also baptized my brothers Ben, Lawrence, Johnny and also Jenny. They were all baptized there at Morges. We looked over the old church, the old cemetery. Ohh it brought back memories.

As a boy I went down those country lanes so many times. But now everything has changed. All the roads are sort of blacktop like, hard blacktop. Back in my day they were gravel or they were sandy, and with our bare feet we could go through it so beautiful. The countryside seemed to change. The trees aren't as big as they used to be. They cut 'em down for logs. Then finally we came around to Morges, then came thru Waynesburg to the old barn. Remember I told you about the old barn? We used to play in there. Well the old barn burned down. There's nothing there but half of the silo. Somebody set fire to it you know, and burned that landmark. That was a famous landmark. That old barn is gone, nothing but weeds there. Ohh, everything is changed. The apple orchard has nothing left but scrubs, the trees all died. Everything is so changed. We came to the hill. We went down to the hill to where we lived. The hill used to be big, but now it's kind of low. Erosion has cut grooves into it, and then they scraped it down and kind of leveled it off and the hill is gone. There's a hill there but not as much.

And all those homes that used to be big block tiles are all cemented over. The government has sold those homes to individual owners. Each built a porch onto the back. We never had a porch onto the back before. They built porches onto the back that are all enclosed. All the houses are covered with cement, like Spanish stucco. We came to the place where we used to live. You couldn't tell my old home from when we lived there! It looks so strange and so different with the hill almost level.

Down by the hill was a great big tree, a walnut tree and that's gone. Oh, everything is just so changed. Pat said, "It's not the way we used to know it when we were boys." But it brought me back a lot of memories from when I was a boy raised in Waynesburg, Ohio. So then we wound our way back to Canton, and I'm here makin' my tape. So I'll stop for now and then there's a few other things I'd like to tell you from when I was a boy.

Well my children I get so emotional when I think of my boyhood days and all my friends who died. Now I'm 76 years old, and how long have I got more in this world before I join my friends and my parents? And as we lost our parents, someday you will lose yours. And, oh I just get kind of choked up. I just don't know what to say. So I'll just close up this tape with my theme song and hope that you will enjoy the tape that I made because all the memories come from the bottom of my heart as I remember them. Goodbye and good luck my dear childrens...

Chapter 9:

Life Lessons Through a Daughter's Eyes

You mustn't get aggravated when your old dad calls you his baby, because he always will think of you as just that – no matter how old or big you may get.

Harry S. Truman, To His Daughter Margaret [16]

The above Harry Truman quote really resonates with me. Growing up as the baby of our family I would squirm as my parents would introduce me to anyone and everyone as their baby. To the waitress. To the checkout lady at the grocery store. To anyone we happened to meet. I would get so embarrassed. Even as an adult mom and dad continued to introduce me to everyone as their baby. Funny though, I didn't mind anymore. In fact, I loved it.

My dad was the best storyteller ever. Countless times when I was shopping with my mom we returned to the meeting spot in the middle of the mall to find him surrounded by strangers. Dad would be moving his hands as he spoke and each and every one of these men were listening in rapt attention. We used to joke about it. Give dad a minute and he got your interest. Every time.

His favorite topics were religion and history. Man oh man, for a guy who only went to school through the sixth grade he was the smartest person I knew. Having gone through twelve years at a Catholic school plus spending each and every Sunday morning at Mass with my parents, sometimes I had a question or two. All I had to do was ask one thing and he was off.

For instance, once when I was about seven years old I asked my dad what heaven is like. He put it in a way a seven-year old would get. I still remember his answer: "In heaven you can eat anything you want. Say you want some gnocchi's. And you think about 'em. Well right there will be a plate of gnocchi's!"

---

16 Harry S Truman, To His Daughter Margaret

Another time when I was a young mom I had an upsetting dream. It was very vivid. In the dream I was shopping with my friend, Cindy. We were best friends during our freshman year of high school and spent many a night at each other's houses. She died suddenly a year after graduation from a severe asthma attack. It was about six months after she died that I had the dream.

As we shopped in my dream, the scene suddenly changed as it often does in dreams. Cindy was now wearing a white robe and a breeze was gently moving her hair and the folds of her robe. She told me that I would die in my early 30's and it would be a tragedy. I still clearly remember, even after all these years have passed what happened next. I said to her "Cindy I can make you say that you're just kidding." Because in your dreams, at least in my dreams I can do that. But I continued, "But I don't want to do that. I want you to tell me, is that true?" She only looked at me with the breeze still blowing her hair. I could not get that dream out of my head.

I remember having many talks with my dad about it and one particular long conversation. He said dreams were symbolic and not to be taken literally. Although I don't remember the details of the rest of that conversation, I do remember that he eased my mind. But I never forgot that dream.

Believe me once I hit birthday number 36 only then did I breathe a sigh of relief.

Dad passed away on January 13, 2001. He taught me a lot in his 94 years. He truly was my mentor. I've selected from my many memories what I consider the ones that had the most profound effect on my life. I call these *Seven Life Lessons Through a Daughter's Eyes*. The seven are faith, love, tradition, gratitude, respect, courage and kindness. Let's explore the 7 lessons together.

Lesson number one: Faith

My dad was the most faithful person I've ever known. He taught by example. None of this *Do what I say, not what I do crap*. And boy did I look up to him. He adhered to the commandments of the Catholic Church and always made sure he did that little bit extra. For instance, he attended Mass every single Sunday and Holy Day of Obligation and even added a daily mass once he was retired from his job at Hercules Engines. He made a retreat every year at Loyola of the Lakes retreat house for forty-four years in a row. Even after he reached the age that the church no longer required fast and abstinence on Fridays he fasted and abstained from meat. He did extra sacrifice throughout his life especially during Lent. He was always available to lend a hand, visit someone in the hospital and provide a kind ear.

But faith goes way beyond what he did at church. He was proud of his church, St. John the Baptist in Canton, Ohio. He was devoted to his faith and loved to talk about it to anyone and everyone who would listen.

Whenever he endured hardships in his life, and believe me there were many, he would offer up the pain and sacrifice to the Lord. He prayed the rosary frequently and not just during adversity. He always prayed for those he loved, for church and world leaders, for the sick, the dying and the dead. Yes he prayed for everyone.

I remember him telling me throughout his life that he prayed for a happy death. I never really understood what he meant by that. At least not until I stood by his bedside and watched as he passed over.

Dad was diagnosed with stomach cancer in the fall of 2000, and three months later it took him. Funny thing, dad had been complaining for a couple of years that there was something wrong with his stomach. He couldn't put his finger on it except that he didn't think he could eat as much. That got a big laugh from us because he still could eat. A lot. When my mom and dad went out to dinner mom always insisted he finish whatever it was that was left on her plate that she couldn't eat. Even if he was full, he would force it down. He'd shake his head and frown but he always, always ate it. Heaven forbid they would waste food. So in the absence of any other symptoms all of us pretty much dismissed his complaints.

In the spring of 2000 dad started to have frequent chest pains. I remember many, many trips to the emergency room. The doctor's were sure that it was his heart. After all, he was 93 years old. He'd had two successful open-heart surgeries at age 71 and 87. Rather than put him through a lot of testing they treated it as such. Dad still insisted that the doctors were missing something that involved his stomach. It was around the same time that my mom was diagnosed with a recurrence of her lung cancer from five years prior. Knowing that they could no longer stay in the apartment they had come to love after leaving their house six years before that, my parents moved into an assisted living facility. A really nice one too thanks to the generosity of two of my brother's financial assistance.

The first week in the new place brought health havoc. My dad threw up blood and quite a lot of it. In the hospital they found a large bleeding ulcer in his stomach. Once they cauterized it he felt much better and seemed to get stronger. I got a phone call from the doctor advising us that dad really needed to have a biopsy done. I talked to my parents and siblings about it. The question was if they found cancer could they do anything? The answer was no so we decided to let it be. It took six months to rupture again, and at that time one look told the tale. Cancer. And quite advanced.

As the days ticked by toward Christmas dad could eat less and less until finally the only thing he could keep down was protein shakes and puddings. Oh how he hated them. But you know what? On Christmas Eve he was able to eat the entire feast and keep it down. Not a huge portion mind you, but he was able to enjoy his favorite meal with his family one last time. What a blessing!

He died on January 13, 2001 at 4:30AM. His wife of 62 years was by his side along with all of his children. He died peacefully. The perfect definition of a happy death. And exactly what he had prayed for all of his life.

Dad never thought he was the perfect Christian. He would point to times when he got irritated like when he had to drive mom to store after store as she shopped for cards. Then she ended up wanting to go back to where she'd seen the first card. To mom cards were very important and they had to say just the right thing. But dad always drove her and never complained to her about it.

It used to drive him crazy when mom would read the newspaper to him. He would be watching TV or reading the paper himself and had to stop frequently so mom could read some interesting tidbit to him. Yet he never told her to stop. He would vent his frustrations to me but he never once snapped at my mom.

During the last few weeks before he died my dad and I had lots of really good conversations. One talk in particular stayed with me. I told him that once he got to heaven if he saw that I was doing something wrong or was on the wrong path he had to tell me, send me a signal or something. I remember what he said next: *"Aww honey, you're better than you think you are."* If I can be one tenth of the man, of the parent, of the Christian my father was, I'm doing okay.

Lesson number two: Love

What is love? When a marriage lasts for sixty-two years until death do them part, that is love.

Growing up my parents were my role models for a loving family. I wasn't around to see the struggles and sacrifices they made with my older siblings as my sister was eleven years older and my three brothers were nine to fifteen years older than I was. But they will all say that our parents worked hard to make sure they never went to bed hungry, gave them a nice Christmas and took them to the ballgames up in Cleveland. They would all say that our parents endured many hardships in the name of love.

All of us saw dad express his love to mom in small ways. He would pull her into a hug and dance her around the room. He left cute little notes around, full of misspellings of course. He let her watch the shows she wanted even if that meant missing the ballgame on TV. He did the dishes and on Sunday he made the sauce. And always there were the cards.

Things were a little easier once the older ones got married and left the house. With just me there at home we were able to go out to eat now and then and even go to an occasional move. Actually we went to the movies only twice to see *Gone with the Wind* and *The Sound of Music*. We went to Meyers Lake Park, a local amusement park once a year and when I was a little older we made the trip to Sandusky, Ohio to Cedar Point. Once we even stayed overnight there in the Breakers Hotel. I went on two vacations with my parents, something my siblings never got to do. When I was twelve we went to New Jersey to visit my brother, Vic, who was in the Air Force. During that trip we went into New York City for the day. The other trip was to Washington DC when I was sixteen.

One of my favorite memories is about Meyers Lake. I loved the carousel. It was a gorgeous thing with handmade wooden horses, really something to see. Every year the park had what was called Nickel Day and all rides were just five cents. That's the day we would go each year, and my dad always bought a fistful of tickets. I absolutely adored the merry-go-round so that's the first place we headed. In fact, I loved it so much that once the ride was over I didn't want to get off the horse. I can still remember my hands holding tightly onto the brass pole, my legs clamped firmly around the saddle. I would lift my little chin and stare defiantly forward. My dad would take one look at me and say to the attendant *"Just let her ride!"* So around and around I went until the last ticket in his stash was used. Then he would pry me off the horse.

Last year Skip and I took a trip to Hartford, Connecticut where the old Meyer's Lake carousel now lives. The town of Hartford made it a focal point in their downtown area of Bushnell Park. It costs $1 to ride. When I saw the old merry-go-round in all its glory for the first time I was moved to tears. I took a ride feeling each beat of the old snare drum as my beautiful stallion glided gracefully up and down. The tears rolled down my cheeks the whole time. It was as if dad were on the sidelines holding those tickets all over again. The only difference was Skip didn't have to pry me off the horse.

I have strived for that love of family in my own life. Dad taught me that you didn't have to spend money to have fun. My kids and I enjoyed many a picnic by the lake where we fed the ducks. We went to the library, read books, played games and did crafts.

Later we were able to buy a motor home. We took lots of beach vacations and built tons of memories. All three of my children have children of their own now. I watch them do many of the same simple things we did when they were young. And more. Mom and Dad would be proud. It makes me smile.

Lesson number three: Tradition

My dad had a strong belief in tradition. He wanted each of his five children to carry on the family unity and various traditions to our own kids. Christmas Eve was my dad's favorite holiday. Growing up Catholic of Italian descent this was always a no-meat meal. Called *The Feast of the Seven Fishes,* the tradition grew out of adherence to the Catholic

Church's rule to abstain from meat on Christmas Eve. The original seven fishes were: squid, tuna, eel, bacala, smelts, sardines and cod. By the time I was old enough to really remember these feasts, bacala, sardines and cod had been cut from the menu and shrimp added. Now we were down to five fishes.

Shortly after that the eel was cut too because nobody ate it except for my dad. It was just gross. The eel looked like a cut up snake parading around a pie plate. Yuck! So now we had four fishes.

The once-a-year meal began with the squid soup. The squid cooks up nice and tender and goes into a tomato-based broth. My mom purchased the squid early in December and she and my dad cleaned them. When I got to be around 14 years old we started to have what we called a Squid Cleaning Party in early December. Let me tell you we cleaned them, and it was no party. Nowadays you can buy cleaned squid with or without the tentacles and they are beautiful. Really lovely.

Back then buying a cleaned squid was unheard of. You got the whole body complete with ugly head and dangling tentacles. When we were all done there was about equal pounds of waste per pound of cleaned squid. The process went like this: Cleaning stations were set up around the old porcelain kitchen table in the basement. Newspapers covered the table and the floor to help sop up some of the excess gunk. Assorted bowls and pans covered the table to catch the good stuff along with the waste. The first step was to pull the heads from the bodies. This was my job, and they were slippery little suckers. The heads went into one bowl and the bodies into another.

Job #2 was to take the body, cut it open with scissors, scoop all the gunk into the waste bowl and throw the body into a separate bowl. The insides contain a piece that looks like clear plastic and lots of goo.

Job #3 was the worst. You had to separate the tentacles from the head, discarding the head into the waste bowl. The tentacles would pile up in yet another bowl and all the little suction cups had to be scraped off. Once scraped, they went into a large pot. I hated that job. I always ended up with the little suction cups under my nails.

Job #4 was to take all of the bodies and scrape the excess slime off with a butter knife. These went into still another bowl where Job #5 took over. Each body was cut up into bite size pieces and thrown into the bowl with the clean tentacles. Once we had a substantial amount of cleaned squid my mom would swap out the large pot for another pot for us to fill. She headed upstairs to the kitchen sink to wash the squid under cold water and put them to soak. She always said you had to wash them until there was no foam left on top of the water. I think she washed them over and over again for twenty four hours. Here's the secret: You can never completely get rid of the foam no matter how many times you wash them!

Once the squid were clean to my picky mother's specifications she froze them until Christmas Eve morning when she made the soup.

The first year us kids took over this job without my parent's assistance we washed them once and that was it. Mom would have had an absolute fit. When the "party" was over we sterilized all the pots, bowls, utensils, table and sink. All the waste was carefully wrapped in multiple layers of newspaper, then bagged and tied and bagged some more before it went into the garbage can in the garage. My dad always said that my mom wrapped garbage like a present. One year my oldest brothers Jim and Lee were given the job to get rid of all the crap. They took the pot that they thought only contained dirty water and emptied it by throwing it into the backyard by the garden. They quickly discovered that the pot was full of squid heads! They flew everywhere which reduced Jim and Lee into fits of laughter. They never told mom but I'll bet all the neighborhood cats had a feast that night.

These days I purchase the frozen "clean" squid in early December like my mom did, but I keep it frozen until early Christmas Eve morning. Nick takes the tentacles and reserves them for later in the day when he fries them up in a tasty coating. They truly are melt in your mouth. Even though the squid (calimari) are prepared two different ways, they only count as one fish. On Christmas Eve morning the squid are washed and cut and put directly into the homemade broth. They only have to cook for about 45 minutes and the finished result is a tender, tasty morsel. Very unlike the pure rubber we ate growing up.

And speaking of rubber…the second course of the menu is the pasta, must be vermicelli. (Vermicelli is very thin spaghetti, just a little thicker than angel hair.) The sauce is put together the day before Christmas Eve almost exactly like it is made any other day with one major exception. There is no meat, no meatballs and no sausage. Instead cans of drained tuna fish are added. Using the tuna in oil will yield a much more flavorful sauce than the tuna in water. The excess oil is skimmed off the top of the sauce (or the soog as my dad called it) as it cooks. Then whole, shelled, hard boiled eggs are added. These need to cook along with the sauce a long time until they get good and rubbery. Oh they are so good, and the rubberier the better! Don't judge it unless you've tried it. We all look forward to this special pasta every year.

The third course consisted of the rest of the various fish along with salad and vegetables. The smelts are fried after a meticulous cleaning. They are a pretty dirty fish. Once I made them for the first time and saw how long it took to gut them and clean them properly I could never eat them again unless I made them. I just couldn't trust that the store-bought variety was really and truly cleaned.

We also had fried shrimp as well as fried breaded cauliflower, broccoli in garlic oil and a tossed salad. Of course a dish of black olives and lupini beans was on the table.

Dessert consisted of fresh fruit, Italian goodies like ponteforte (Kind of like Italian fruit cake), Torrones (an Italian nougat candy), ceci and fava (pronounced *Cheech* and *Fow,* a dried and salted garbanzo and lima bean), nuts in their shells (Hazelnuts aka filberts, almonds, walnuts and Brazil nuts) and homemade cookies. Later on my brother, Lee always made the egg nog. But before we all got up from the table there were two important traditions that took place.

The first was the burning of the Brazil nut. My dad would take a whole Brazil nut that he had cracked and readied for this moment. He lit the end of it and told the following story as the nut burned:

> *"My dad always would tell us boys not to eat too many of these here Brazil Nuts because they are full of oil and will give you a stomach ache". To demonstrate this dad would light the nut on fire, and hold it up so we could see it slowly burning. "See here, it burns just like a candle."*

Every year at our Christmas Eve table my youngest son, Nick does the burning of the Brazil nut.

The second tradition was the peeling of the orange. My dad had an unusual way of peeling an orange. He did it with his teeth. As a child whenever I needed an orange peeled I'd just give it to dad and lightning quick he peeled it. It was funny to watch. As fast as his mouth filled up with orange peels he let them drop out of his mouth. He could peel an orange in ten seconds or less. All of his grandkids got a kick out of watching him do this and somehow it became part of the end of our meal. We have many a video capturing this crazy stunt.

Now at my family's table Nick has taken over this event. He does a good job too and all the little kids have their eyes glued on the spectacle.

Yes, it was quite a feast and still is. After my parents passed away all of us kids held their own version of *The Feast* with our own families. We've tweaked the various fish over the years. This past Christmas Eve we went back to seven fishes which were: Squid soup, Fried Calamari (Same fish counts only as one), Tuna sauce, Fried Smelt, Fried Shrimp, Mussels and finally a Lobster and Crab dip. It is and will always be the most anticipated meal of the year even before Thanksgiving.

And speaking of Thanksgiving, I have so many wonderful memories of that day. After I got married I took over hosting Thanksgiving for my parents and my two uncles. Our menu was traditional for us but quite a bit different from the average meal. Along with the turkey and dressing there would be wedding soup, mashed potatoes and gravy, candied sweet potatoes, Irish potatoes, breaded cauliflower, broccoli in garlic oil, cranberry salad, cranberry sauce, tossed salad and lemons for the turkey. Of course there was the ever present dish of black olives. Dessert was pumpkin and pecan pie.

The first thing I cut from the menu was the wedding soup because it just wasn't needed. We always had it on Christmas Day anyway. The mashed potatoes were added as that was something that my mom hardly ever made. I'll never forget the look on Skip's face the first time he shared our Thanksgiving meal and there were no mashed potatoes and gravy on the table. He never said a word but needless to say he spoke up the next year. The pan stuffing was another addition. I cannot imagine growing up that we had enough stuffing to go around with just what was in the bird. We all love it so Skip makes the pan stuffing and it is fantastic.

I dropped the tossed salad from the menu because I thought we had plenty of vegetables. My mom was the one that made the cranberry salad every year, so after she died it fell from the menu too. One of these years I will surprise my kids by adding it back. David especially loved it. The Irish potatoes were my dad's favorite thing so I will always keep them on the menu. They are roasted alongside the turkey and really are unique and quite good.

I made Thanksgiving dinner each and every year until this past one when I passed the baton to Nick and Hallie. It was bittersweet giving up that day but I decided it was time. Nick really wanted Brady to grow up like he did being able to smell the succulent roasting turkey aroma first thing when he woke up. And what a fine turkey dinner they provided! Karrie took over making the pan stuffing and it was every bit as good as Skip's if not better!

My parents really enjoyed coming to my house for Thanksgiving dinner. They appreciated that I included my dad's brothers, Patsy and Lawrence every year. It wouldn't have been Thanksgiving without them. I remember one year that I roasted the Irish potatoes a little too long. They were on the crunchy side to say the least. Every time my dad or one of my uncles crunched away as they gnawed on that potato, well let's just say I can hear it even now. I also couldn't make eye contact with any of my kids or we would have been rolling on the floor.

On Thanksgiving Day 2000, my dad knew that it would be his last Thanksgiving. It was bittersweet. He died on January 13, 2001 followed by mom on April 17, 2001. When Thanksgiving 2001 arrived the dinner was a somber affair. After everybody left I drove to the cemetery and left at their grave site a turkey leg and a potato for my dad and a candied sweet potato for my mom, their favorites. Crazy I know but somehow it made me feel better.

A funny thing happened. Let me set the scene by explaining another tradition that I shared with my dad. When I was growing up a Sunday custom was to take a drive to the cemetery to visit the graves of both sets of grandparents. The driveway leading into the cemetery itself was lined with oak trees. My dad and I had a race to see who could count the most squirrels. *"There's one! There's one!"* we each would shout, craning our necks, both of us hoping we would be the one to have the higher tally. You know I still count the squirrels.

So that Thanksgiving morning when I arrived at the grave site I was shocked to find two squirrels sitting quietly by mom and dad's tombstone. They never moved as I approached, said my prayer and finally left. I'm sure they enjoyed the feast I left! The funny thing is I had never before or since seen a squirrel at the grave site.

Oh we had lots of traditions: Spaghetti dinner on Sundays, greeting cards on holidays, Sunday drives, pasta beans on Fridays, individually wrapped ice cream treats, bunny cookies, raisin bread and ricotta pie on Easter, sausage and peppers at midnight on Christmas Eve, dividing up my Halloween candy, weekly visits, oh so many memories. One of my favorites was going to the dump with my dad when I was a little girl. As we drove up and down the hills he always would say, *"Now we're on the roller coaster, we're going up the hill, up, up, up. We're at the top; here we go, down, down, down the hill!"* Oh how I loved that! My daughter has the same memory because grandpa took her to the dump and they rode that roller coaster together.

Once my siblings started having families of their own my dad started the tradition of a family picnic every summer. It was so important to both of my parents that the family stayed close and saw each other often. Family was everything, and my dad spoke of it often. We still get together, all sixty-some of us twice a year for a family party. I'm sure it makes my dad smile.

Lesson number four: Gratitude

Dad was a humble man. He never asked for things for himself. The life he led alongside my mother for sixty-two years was a simple one. Their entertainment was going out to eat and that wasn't all that often. Growing up we always went out on two special occasions: Easter and Mother's Day, both times directly after Mass. It wasn't until I got a little older, maybe 12 or 13 that we went out occasionally, maybe once a month. Always frugal, they preferred the buffet type restaurants where my dad could really get his fill.

Dad led the blessing before every meal. *Bless us oh Lord, for these thy gifts which we are about to receive, from thy bounty through Christ our Lord, Amen.* Before. Every. Meal.

My parents taught us to be grateful for our time together especially at mealtime. We always gathered around the kitchen table as a family to eat. Always. This is a habit that I continued while raising my family. I believe the dinner table is an important part of building family unity. Even when we were crazed living our lives around baseball, football and endless practices we came together to eat.

I mentioned before about greeting cards and how important they were to my mom. Dad knew this and always got her a card for every occasion. They were always nice, but the best thing about them was always his own message that he added beneath the printing. Written in his halting penmanship complete with horrible spelling, the words came straight from his heart. And each little note on every single card over the years always contained the same two words somewhere within. Those two words were thank you.

He thanked my mom for giving him five wonderful "childrens" (as he called them), for walking alongside him for all the years, for putting up with him. He shared his gratitude for meals and smiles and companionship. Dad wasn't ashamed to express his gratitude. He was thankful in all things.

My dad is the one who really taught me about being grateful in all situations. And that is a subject that isn't all that simple to grasp. It's easy to be thankful during the good times when everybody is healthy, the job is going well and finances are in order. But when life throws you a curve ball and now you're dealing will illness, injury, accidents or unexpected calamities including too much month left after the paycheck is gone, well that's another thing altogether.

Over the years dad would weave the concept of gratitude into our talks. He would use a story from the life of Christ as an example to make any point he wanted, to answer any question or problem I had. His comparisons were endless and they always made perfect sense. I walked away from every discussion (and yes at times I referred to them as sermons) with plenty of food for thought.

He not only talked to me about being grateful, he showed me. He delighted in being able to take a nap after his retirement, remembering those many years when that was a luxury out of his reach. He was content to spend night after night at home just watching TV or listening to music never for a second feeling like he was missing out on something. He was joyful in his quiet time spent reading and taught me the wonders of the written word. But he was happiest when he was in the midst of his family.

Even though my parents had been gone over nine years when my son, Nick, was burned in that freak accident in July 2010, I drew comfort from my father's example. His words helped form my prayers. His example supported me. His faith provided the basis of my own faith which sustained me. Without that faith, despair would have been just a breath away.

Thank you mom and dad for all of your sacrifices, for all the little things you did for your family each and every day. I probably never told you that, but I'm telling you now and I believe you know my heart. My cup runneth over.

Lesson number five: Respect

I was taught from an early age about respect. I was never allowed to call an adult by their first name, I was to sit quietly when the adults were talking, I was to say thank you for anything given to me whether I liked it or not.

While that may seem quite different from today's world, my mom and dad had a great deal of respect for their own parents. They both pitched in and helped by working at an early age and turning over their earnings to the family. They didn't consider this a hardship either as they were quite willing to do their part in the name of respect. And love. Some of the stories I've shared in the earlier chapters demonstrate this.

Both of my parents came from large families, seven siblings for my dad and nine for my mom. That meant lots of visiting. During these visits I was allowed one cookie. If my aunt would offer me another one I would steal a look at my mom to see if it was ok. Sometimes my aunt would say *"Don't look at your mother! Take another cookie!"* My mom would laugh and nod her head, and only then would I reach for the second cookie. Sometimes she would kick me under the table. I remember one time when I was feeling a bit feisty I said loudly *"Why are you kicking me?"* Oh boy did I get it later.

We visited my grandparents every single Sunday. These were my dad's folks. My mom's father died before I was born, and her mother died when I was only three. I don't remember her. Had they been alive we would have visited them too. That was one of the ways my parents showed respect for their parents, by visiting regularly.

All of my grandparents immigrated to this country from Italy so they spoke no English. I remember sitting quietly Sunday after Sunday as the adults talked in Italian. I only knew they were talking about me when I heard my grandmother say *"Moddy-on"*, her Italian version of *Maryanne*. My grandpa died when I was eight so my memories of him are mostly of him sitting in a chair and squeezing a ball or sitting at the kitchen table. Grandma died when I was fifteen. Those were two of the very few times I ever saw my dad cry.

When I was still living at home my siblings would visit every Sunday, and we always had spaghetti. As the grandchildren started to arrive, all the little cousins looked forward to Sundays and spaghetti at Grandma and Grandpa's house. Eventually I grew up and I had a family. My kids loved those Sunday afternoons.

We also showed respect for my father by honoring his faith. One special tradition involved bringing him a palm leaf on Palm Sunday. My brothers got fancy and wove the palm into crosses, something I still cannot do. Dad would take all of these palms and spread them around the house to accent the crucifix's that hung in each room. I do that now too around my house. I still think of dad on Palm Sunday, and I make sure to take his palm to the grave site.

Both of my parents had a terrific work ethic. No rest until the work was done. My parents used to make a little extra money by cleaning buildings in the evenings. I was probably about eight years old when they started doing this. They cleaned an office building and a dentist's office. My job was to empty the wastebaskets and ashtrays. Once that was done I was allowed to play. I would sit at the desks and pretend I worked there. One desk in particular always had snacks in the drawers. Of course I helped myself. If my parents had known this I would have been in trouble.

The basement in the dentist's office was a scary place. There was this long, narrow corridor that turned into an alcove. There in that niche was a group of wheelchairs. It was very dark. I would force myself to creep down that passageway all the way to the end. Once I saw the wheelchairs I ran back as fast as I could. Only then did I allow myself to play "secretary".

My dad put in a full day of work at the factory and then had to put in a couple of hours more at the buildings. What a sacrifice that was. I'm sure all he wanted was to be able to sit down in his chair and relax. They finally gave up the buildings when I was around twelve. That was when my mom got a job working at a small family-owned dry cleaner shop. It was close enough that she walked there while my dad was at work and I was at school. Then dad would pick her up when she was done at 6PM. That was when I started to help prepare our supper. I liked it so much that I started to experiment with new recipes. I still enjoy doing that.

I also have a good work ethic, something I developed by watching my parents. Being respectful of time and the job was always important to dad, and it's important to me too.

I watched my parents put their duty to their job and their employers first even when they didn't feel good. Imagine having to leave the house at 5:30 every morning and go to a job you don't like where it is hot, noisy and grueling. Then knowing that when you get home you only have a couple of hours before you have to go and spend two or three hours cleaning up someone else's mess. Then do it all over again the next day. Every day, every week, same thing.

Dad retired when I was a junior in high school after spending forty-three years at his factory job. That's when he started to enjoy his days doing gardening, building bird houses and tinkering in his wood shed. He built some pantry cupboards that I especially liked. In fact, when I got my own house I asked him to build me one. He did and included a note on the inside *"Fore my baby, love dad."* I preserved that note and it still hangs on the inside of the door of that cupboard to this day.

When my brother's built their own house, he painted all the rooms. Mine too. When something needed fixing, we called dad. He could do most anything. But he is especially known for the nativity crèche's he built. He would go for walks in the woods to collect bark and twigs. Everyone loved the finished product so much that he made one for each of his and mom's siblings. Each of his children got one, the oldest grandchild in each family as well as his four granddaughters. My daughter has her own which she cherishes. My boys both are eying mine.

Yes, my dad showed respect for everyone he met regardless of whether or not he knew them or agreed with them. And everyone respected my dad for his diplomacy, his kindness and gentle nature. And that is the thing that I think would make him the most proud. The fact that he earned the respect of others while living what he considered to be a simple life.

Lesson number six: Courage

How often do we have the opportunity to be courageous? Some might think that being brave only applies to big events that make the news. Like the men who ran headlong into the surf to rescue the children from the van that their mother purposely drove into the Atlantic ocean in Daytona Beach. Or the teachers that faced down the gunman at Sandy Hook Elementary School and ended up giving their lives. Or all the brave souls that were on site on 9/11.

Anyone fighting cancer is definitely courageous. Skip shows bravery every day as he fights past the pain from his Parkinson's disease and chronic daily headaches. You wouldn't always know it either as he always has a big smile on his face.

Nick had tremendous courage as he faced the four grueling skin graft surgeries after his freak accident that left him burned 46% of his body. His attitude and perseverance was a source of inspiration for everyone that knew him and many that did not. And right beside him the whole way was Hallie with her steadfastness and silent courage.

But courage also exists in the will to stand up to someone who disagrees with you or worse yet is a bully. Kids all across America face this at school every day. But adults can also be bullies. Standing up to bullies can be done with kindness as long as there is firmness. Standing up for something you believe in is an important skill to cultivate and demonstrate, especially to your own kids.

As a boy, dad showed his mettle with some of the crazy stunts he pulled like jumping the trains and climbing that smokestack. He may not have shown the best judgment but he sure was no pushover either.

My dad showed courage throughout his entire life especially in the face of illness. He never showed fear although I'm sure at times he felt fearful. He never questioned why me? His attitude was always acceptance and willingness to give the sacrifice up to the Lord. Although I witnessed firsthand dad's strength after having back surgery and two open-heart surgeries, the event I will always remember is how he faced the diagnosis of terminal stomach cancer.

We were hit with this devastating news in November 2000. At this same time my mom was weakening from her lung cancer. Dad's doctor said he would need to get blood every couple of weeks as the cancer would cause anemia, or the loss of red blood cells. At first dad resisted this saying with a rueful smile, *"I'll take the short form!"* In other words, he didn't want to do anything to prolong the inevitable. But we asked him to please get the blood so he could have one last Christmas with the family. Dad agreed and we had a beautiful albeit bittersweet holiday.

Dad was lucid and talkative almost until the end. Every morning he would wake up and say *"Doggone it, I'm still here!"*

We had so many wonderful conversations, and I will forever cherish these special times with dad.

I had watched him show courage when he lost his parents and four brothers so I knew what was ahead for me. Realistically I thought I knew what was ahead, but until you lose a loved one you really don't know. Yes, my parents were 94 and 87 years old respectively when they died and I was lucky to have them until I was 46 years old. But they were still my parents and I grieved.

I feel fortunate that I had my parents as my role models in life.

Lesson number seven: Kindness

It's one thing to be nice; it's another to be kind. Demonstrated throughout the telling of dad's boyhood stories are simple acts of kindness. Yes, I know he was quite ornery too!

Remember the story of little Bruno? Some of the other kids were quick to criticize the boy for not going to school yet still playing outside. Dad defended Bruno to the whole class.

I grew up watching my parents do so many small acts of thoughtfulness and consideration. Mom would always cook for someone who was sick. She had the fixin's for wedding soup in her freezer at all times and taught me to do the same. Her reasoning was if someone died she could deliver soup to the grieving family very quickly.

They always brought canned fruit to someone recuperating from a surgery or illness. A couple of large cans of peaches and fruit cocktail always rounded out whatever other goodies they brought. We kind of made a joke about that over the years, *don't forget the fruit cocktail!*

Another wonderfully kind gesture I observed my whole life was my parents going to calling hours. Mom and dad went for everybody. They read the obituaries in the paper and made sure to pay a visit if a loved one, friend or acquaintance lost someone close to them. They drummed into my head that you go to the calling hours for the one who is grieving. It isn't necessary that you knew the deceased person at all because you are there to support the one left behind. Until you are in the position of receiving this kindness it may be hard for you to grasp.

I want to share a story with you that epitomizes the virtue of kindness. When my daughter, Marcy, was twelve she participated in the Miss Pre-Teen USA pageant. It was something she had always wanted to do. I have to tell you though, boy were we bumpkins! My little girl looked like a pretty little twelve year old with her long hair and age-appropriate clothing. I was amazed at some of the stage moms and bug-eyed over the getups some of the girls wore. *And the make-up!*

For her talent Marcy played *Let There Be Peace on Earth* on the piano. She did a fine job but it was no comparison to some of the talent acts that graced the stage. The plethora of agents and choreographers that accompanied many of the contestants was mind-boggling.

She didn't make the top ten which was fine, she was just so happy to have fulfilled her dream. The pageant took place in Cleveland, Ohio which was about one hour from our house. A few friends and family members came to the pageant and joined us in our hotel room afterwards.

Everyone was there when my friend, Kay* and her husband, Dwight* arrived a little late. (*Not their real names) Kay's family didn't approve of her marriage because Dwight was black. But they were very happy together. Kay had been shut off from her parents and the rest of her family since the marriage, and this little gathering was the first time she came face-to-face with them.

I answered her knock on the door, gave them a hug and invited them in. I still remember the smiles frozen on their faces as all conversation in the room ceased. Everyone was on the other side of the room as Kay and Dwight just stood there. I didn't know what to do!

Just then my dad walked across the room and extended his hand saying, *"Hi, I'm Victor DiCola"*. They visibly relaxed as they shook his hand and proceeded to have an animated conversation with him. That loosened everybody up. Although her parents didn't talk to her, everyone else did.

I was so proud of my father in that moment. If my father was in the room he absolutely would not allow someone to be ostracized or made to feel uncomfortable. We can all take a lesson from him. He was quite a man.

I know that I have never deliberately hurt anyone but I'm a far cry from the person my father was. I also know that I can take a lesson from my father's ability to turn the other cheek in some situations. I'll just say that I'm a work in progress.

Children learn by what they see. My parents were good role models and I hope that my own children and grandchildren will live by that example.

Another lesson of kindness was delivered by my extended Italian family when we visited Italy in 1994. It truly was the trip of a lifetime. My daughter along with my parents and my brother, Jim and his family visited both of my parent's home towns.

We started in Longi which is in Sicily. This is the birthplace of my mother's parents, Leone Vitale and Francesca Pidala. We stayed with my mother's cousins, Paulo and Franga Zingales for a whirlwind 4 full days and 3 nights. Mom's dad and Franga's dad, Frank, were brothers. They have a beautiful 4-story house, typical for the area. They have their own little grocery store right there. Longi is very picturesque with narrow cobblestone streets and tall, narrow houses all built on the side of the mountain. There is a terrace on each floor. It felt like I was really in Italy. Their daughter, Annamarie met us at the house along with her 11-year old son, Ferdi who is fluent in 3 languages!

So, so many relatives came to the house to visit us over the course of those 4 days, relatives from both the Vitale and the Pidala families. We even went with the Pidala clan for a feast one afternoon complete with music and dancing. I actually filmed the frantic tarantella and singing that took place. We had such fun.

We took a trip to the cemetery and I saw my great-grandparents graves. All were above the ground and adorned with their photograph. Very ornate and beautiful.

One of my mother's relatives we got to see quite often was Francesco Pidala. His father and my mother's mother were brother and sister. Francesco presented me with a huge bag of hazelnuts. We had been enjoying them fresh from the trees so I was excited about this gift. Unfortunately we were not permitted to bring them out of the country. In fact on the mini-bus trip to the airport they actually spilled out of the back of the van rolling everywhere. This of course reduced us to fits of giggles and the driver was glad to be rid of us.

As we made our way from Sicily to Rome and finally to the next leg of our journey, my dad's hometown roots, I reflected on how grateful I was to have been given the opportunity to visit my heritage with my parents by my side. The hospitality and kindness of our relatives took my breath away. We were virtual strangers yet they treated us like family who had never really been gone. What a blessing.

Our next stop was Roccaraso, a little town in the foothills of the mountains and ski slopes about one hour outside of Rome. Here we spend 3 full days and 2 nights. The town of Roccaraso was actually leveled by the Germans during World War II and had been mostly rebuilt. How thrilling to stand in front of what was left of my great-grandparents home alongside my father! My ancestors actually walked these same streets!

Again we visited the local cemetery and viewed many of our relative's grave sites. As in Longi, they were above ground with photographs.

We visited with our cousins who owned the Marimonte Hotel. Funny story. As our cousins Tito, Rinaldo and Aqualine took us on a detailed tour of the kitchen and dining room I spotted a cluster of cute little pitchers that were printed with the words, "Roccaraso Marimonte". I was filming with my video camera and zoomed in on those pitchers. I made quite a fuss over them. Soon Aqualine picked up two and now I was literally prancing. He presented one to Jim who doesn't understand and I have to tell him that it's a gift! I am so sure that the second one is for me or my mother that I reached for it. Aqualine pulled it back. Instead he gave it to Jim with the instruction to portare (carry) it to America for their dear friend, Piadine. I was crushed.

What makes this story especially funny is later when we return home and replay the video, my voice drastically changes from an excited lilt to a depressed monotone during the "pitcher caper". Jim later tells me how bad he felt that I didn't get my own pitcher. In fact, just last year he gave me the coveted *Marimonte* pitcher which holds a place of honor in my home.

Again all of us were shown so much kindness from our extended family. And what a joy it was watching my father interact with his relatives! One of the most touching moments of the trip was as I observed my father saying goodbye to them on the morning of our departure. As he hugged them, there were tears in his eyes and a bit of a tremble to his lip. That did me in and I cried. I never felt closer to my parents than I did on this glorious trip.

The trip ended in the heart of Italy, St. Peter's Basilica in Rome. We were among a smaller indoor audience of about 3500 people to see the pope, Pope John Paul II. We received the papal blessing and it was a moving moment. To witness the root of my family's faith alongside my parents was truly the highlight of the trip.

These seven lessons sum up the reasons why my father was my mentor, and still is even though he's gone. Who in your life do you admire? Have you told them? If you haven't, do it now. After all, now is the only time that we have.

Chapter 10:

To Josephine

My father didn't tell me how to live; he lived, and let me watch him to it.
Clarence Kelland [17]

Victor's famous angel story belongs in this chapter dedicated to his loving wife, Josephine.

Angelwhisper's were always present in Victor's life, and they can be heard in your life if you just stop and listen....

His name was Victor. Throughout all of his 88 years he had believed in angels, and on February 14, 1994 that belief became a reality for his family.

Victor and his wife Josephine had just returned from dinner to celebrate Valentine's Day. Yes, after fifty-five years of marriage, they still celebrated Valentine's Day every year with a nice dinner. That particular year after returning home, they were sitting quietly at the kitchen table. Josephine was watching over him worriedly because Victor was experiencing chest pain. "Just a little pressure", he insisted. "Let's see if it gets better", he said. Josephine anxiously wringing her hands was close to tears. Just then the phone on the wall over her shoulder rang. She answered it and the voice on the other end said "This is 9-1-1, do you have an emergency?" Confused, Josephine could only say "What?" The 911 operator repeated: "This is 9-1-1, do you have an emergency?" Josephine said to Victor, "It's 9-1-1, They want to know if we have an emergency." Victor immediately responded. "That's my angel! Tell them I need an ambulance!" Josephine then told 9-1-1 that her husband was having chest pain and an ambulance was sent immediately.

What followed was a series of "coincidences" that can only be

---

17 Clarence Kelland

explained as miraculous. The end result was an 88-year old man having triple bypass heart surgery against great odds. He went on to live six more years. He went on an Alaskan cruise with his wife. He went to Italy with his family. He saw a World Series game. He enjoyed countless family weddings, dinners and get-togethers. Quality of life? In spades! When he finally passed away in 2001, it wasn't his heart that took him.

We just had a most memorable week. We celebrated our 45th wedding anniversary, and the children took us out for a wonderful dinner. In the morning we went to church at St. Paul's, all my grandchildren, all her sisters and brothers, my sisters and brothers and a few friends gathered at the church. Then we went to the Pines for a wonderful dinner, and we had a wonderful time. I'll never forget, thank you my children for being so thoughtful. Mother, she just really enjoyed that very, very much.

Then a week later we celebrated mom's 70th birthday. They surprised us. They told us all kinds of lies. It was supposed to be a political party for our nephew, Sammy Purses who was running for Mayor of Canton. But, here instead they had all gathered together, all the family, our brothers and sisters and friends. When we walked into that hall they all start singing Happy Birthday. Mom she was all choked up, she didn't hardly eat anything. All my grandchildren and everybody was all hugging and kissing. That is something I will cherish and remember for the rest of my life. Thank you my dear children. That made a wonderful day for your mother and made me very, very happy. I'll never forget all the wonderful things that you have done.

Jo, these are a few words for you although I'm reading it from a card:

> *You are my beauty in my world, the joy in my heart the meaning in my life, you are my love.*

I remember my parents always exchanging cards for every holiday. Every one. They didn't buy each other gifts. But the cards meant a lot to my mother. She took a long time selecting them too. The words had to be just right. Then she would add her own few personal words at the bottom. I still have some and I treasure them. My dad also would add his own personal message at the

bottom of his cards too. We always got a kick out of his messages. He was a horrible speller, and sometimes it took some effort to decipher his words. But regardless his message was always heartfelt.

The very last card my father ever gave my mother was Christmas 2000. I have the original card framed and hanging in my bedroom. His personal message to my mom that he hand printed on the bottom is as follows:

Dear Jo
The Day I Maried You
Was The Most Happy
Day Of My Life
I Loved You
Then
And
Love You Now To The Last Sun Set
Of My Life. So. Be Happy. We Will
Be Togetter In Heaven Where
Love. Never. Ends
Vic Your Rigth. Hand. Man
Fater. Son. Holey Sprit

Now children a few words about your mother. You know, she always says, "I'm not good like you, you go to church every day. You're going' to heaven, I don't know about me." I say, "Jo, God has got a special place for you. You have done more good than you know. You've been a wonderful wife, a wonderful mother, a wonderful person. You'd take the shirt off your back, if you had a shirt. I should say you would take your blouse. That's what a generous person you are. You're always doing for others. You're thinking' about others, you're never thinking' about yourself. You knew nothing in your life but work, every day. Now God will welcome you with open arms. You have given me five wonderful children. The Lord will say, 'Look what you have done. You have brought five wonderful children into this world'. And they have blessed me with thirteen wonderful grandchildren. What more treasure than that could a person ask? And God will look down on you and smile and say 'Welcome, My faithful servant, for such is the kingdom of heaven'." Mom would say "Oh no, Vic, you're just saying that, I'm not that good." Jo, don't belittle yourself. Everybody thinks a lot of you, you are a wonderful person. To me you're tops.

Yes Jo, you're all I need to see me through to make my life worthwhile, to brighten all my days and make me smile. That's for you Jo.

Hearing music was all it took for mom to get her feet a-dancing. You put one of those polka's on or a Tarantella, and her and her sister's Sitsi Frances and Clara and Jenny, oh the times we had at old weddings and stuff. She really, really enjoyed it.

Yes Jo, those were the happy days when you used to dance raising a family. Now you're 70 years old. You can look back and be glad it's all over. No, we're not glad it's all over. I'd like to have small ones all over again. But it's not to be. So I will play one more song while you are still in a dancing mood, then I'll recite the last poem on this card for mom.

Happy Anniversary and Happy Birthday to you Dear Jo. And here is the last of my little poems which I will dedicate to you:

You're all I need to share my hopes, the dreams I'm dreaming of.
You're all I need to be happy, all I need to love.

That's the end of this recording for today I'll come back at a later date and try to fill the tape with other things that happens in our lives. So for awhile God bless you and keep you.

Dear Jo, today on June 18, 1988 we celebrate our 50th golden anniversary of our marriage. I know we had a good marriage. I love you just as much as I did that first day. We are blessed with a wonderful family and grandchildrens and on this day I dedicate this group of inspirational music. It comes from my heart, the music can say it better than I could, words that I listen to, meditate. We gotta thank our Lord for all the good things he has blessed us with throughout these 50 years.

I know we had ups and downs. We had good times, and we had bad times. But we took 'em all in stride. We trust in the Lord, and the Lord repaid us back in many ways. We had 5 wonderful children, 13 beautiful grandchildren; I should say handsome grandchildren, and a great granddaughter.

Now Jo, I'm not much for words, to talk about love and all that. But I may do something sometime and get you mad, but I mean well. I hope God will give us a few more years to see us through. Our children are having a little party on us, and won't tell us all the details of it. But that's alright. We appreciate everything they're doing for us. We're all getting together to have a party there and have a good time. The date today is June 19, 1988. We will go to the St. John Hall after the Mass. We trust in God for all the blessings he has given us. That's all we have to say for now. Good bye.

Selection of Music...

"...Life is fading fast away, love my darling will be, always young and fair to me yes my darling, always young and fair to me... growing old, silver threads among the gold, shine upon my brow today.. life is fading fast away..." [18]

(Those lyrics really choke me up...)

Well childrens, this is about the end of my story, I'm back again for the last time. The tape is about done now. All of my friends are gone, the old horse is gone, the dog is gone, and the cat's gone, everything is gone.

I don't remember much more, unless I start repeating. Some of my things, I could go into bigger details and enlarge every instance that I have told you, but it would take too much tape. Everything I told you was in brief. So with that I'm gonna sign off this tape, it's just about winding down, and of course I'll close up with my theme song again, *My Treasure*.

And God Bless you all my children, and I hope you will enjoy these tapes after I'm long gone. Maybe this will be a memory that I'm still talkin' to you, and it's a wonderful gift to have. I wish I would have had something like this of my dad, all the stories he used to tell of all the things I used to do when I was a little child and all the hardships he told

---

18   From the song, Silver Thread Among the Gold, By Daniel O'Donnell

me about himself. He had a lot of hard times. What I'm telling you now he told me about his boyhood, how rough he had it. And oh, he had it rough. So now I'm going to put on my theme song. Goodbye and God bless you.

Until we Meet Again, So Long.

Chapter 11:

Recipes

Mange! Mange!

Wedding Soup

Make one large pot of chicken broth using 2 large chicken breasts with skin. Once broth is done remove chicken and strain. When chicken is cool enough to handle, break into bite-size pieces discarding skin and add meat back to broth.

Clean 4 heads endive. Immerse in pot of salted water and let cook until tender. Strain, cut into small pieces. Add to broth.

The little meatballs that go into this soup are made the same way you would make meatballs for spaghetti except they are very small. 1 LB of hamburger will make enough meatballs for a large pot of soup. Combine the hamburger with one egg, black pepper, garlic powder, celery salt, oregano and Progresso bread crumbs. Mix well and shape into small balls. This is time consuming and mine are not as small and perfect as Mom's always were! Originally Mom would brown these in a skillet before adding them to the broth. Then one of her sisters told her to just put them on a cookie sheet and broil them. What a time saver! So do that! Watch them close because it doesn't take long. Remove and add them to broth.

Turn the pot on low to let the flavors meld. Add salt to taste and Romano cheese. The last thing is to add the eggs. Hardboil them ahead of time, then just cut into small pieces into the soup. Some people prefer to add raw eggs to the soup to make an eggdrop. But Mom always preferred the hardboiled eggs and so do I.

If you want to make it ahead to freeze, package the meatballs, endive and broth with chicken pieces in it separately. Then throw it all together when you're ready adding eggs at the end just like you do when you make it fresh.

Squid Soup

2 pks frozen cleaned squid
1/4 C Olive oil
2 medium onions
3 garlic cloves
Black pepper, celery salt, fresh parsley, salt to taste
1/2 C Romano cheese
1-15 oz can tomato sauce
1-12 oz can tomato paste

Saute onions and garlic in olive oil. Discard cloves. Add seasoning. Fill dutch oven about 2/3 full with water and add tomato sauce, tomato paste and onion/seasoning mix with oil. Add cleaned squid pieces and bring to boil. Reduce heat and simmer 45 minutes to 1 hour. Add grated Romano cheese at the end.

Gnocchi

5 LB potatoes
9 C flour PLUS 1 C in rolling
2 tsp salt
1 egg

Boil potatoes with skins, do not add more salt. Peel while still warm. Using a potato ricer, mash potatoes and add salt and egg. Add 4 C flour. Turn dough over but Do Not Knead. Add 3 C more flour and turn dough again. Then add final 2 C flour and continue mixing. Don't let it stand too long as it will get sticky. Cut a hunk of dough and roll in flour with fingers into long roll. Cut individual gnocchi with knife, dip into flour and place on wax paper lined cookie sheet. Freeze until dry then bag them for later use. To cook: Bring pot of water to full boil, add a little salt and olive oil. Add gnocchi and DO NOT STIR until they rise to the top. When they come up to the top use a wooden spoon to life from side to bottom.

Pasta Fagioli (Pasta Beans)

3-4 garlic cloves
Olive oil
1 tsp Celery salt
1/2 tsp Black pepper
1-6 oz can tomato paste
2 cans Navy beans
1 LB Ditilini pasta
Grated Romano cheese

Brown garlic in olive oil, then discard the clove. Add tomato paste to the olive oil and cook, stirring constantly. It will darken in color. Meanwhile, empty the 2 undrained cans of bean into a sauce pan. Pour the cooked tomato paste and oil into the beans and stir, set aside. Cook pasta as usual. When it is done, strain about half of the water keeping the other half in reserve. Add the tomato paste and beans mixture directly into the pasta and water. If too watery you can add additional reserved water. Add Romano cheese and cover. Cook on low for about 20 minutes.

We always served this two dishes at a time. Eat one while the other cools. Dad always experiments with different pasta shapes. His favorite was to make a double batch with one pound ditalini and one pound small shells.

Irish Potatoes

Peel small sized potatoes and leave whole. Soak 15 minutes in cold water. Mix 1/2 C grated Romano cheese with 1 Tbl oregano. Dip each potato into the cheese mixture then place alongside the turkey to roast for the last 2 hours of cooking time. Enjoy!

Bunny Cookies

4 C sifted flour
1 C butter, room temperature
1 C sugar
2 eggs, beaten
1 tsp vanilla
3 Tbl milk
1 tsp baking soda

Cut flour and butter together, set aside. Add sugar to beaten eggs and mix well. Add to flour mixture. Mix together, vanilla, milk and baking soda and add to flour mixture. Chill 2 hours. Roll and cut with bunny cookie cutter. Bake 8-10 min at 350 degrees. When cool ice with white frosting. Decorate ears and tail with coconut, use a raisin for the eye.

Ricotta Pie

Use glass pie plate to make 2 pie crusts:
3/4 C Crisco
2 1/4 C flour
2 Tbl sugar
1 beaten egg
2 tsp baking powder
1/4 tsp salt
1/2 C milk.
Bake crust for 10 minutes at 400 degrees.

Filling for 2 pies:
2 LB Ricotta cheese
2 eggs
1/8 tsp vanilla
13 oz grated milk chocolate*
Combine and fill crusts. Bake for 45 minutes at 350 degrees. *If you like a more chocolate flavor, use dark chocolate. Feel free to increase the amount of chocolate for your taste.

Raisin Bread

2 C raisins
Hot water
3 oz dry yeast
1 C water
2 Tbl sugar PLUS 3 1/4 C sugar
1/2 C sifted flour PLUS 15 C sifted flour
1 LB butter, melted
1 C milk
12 jumbo eggs
2 tsp vanilla
1 tsp salt

Soak 2 C raisins in hot water until plump. Dissolve 3 oz dry yeast in 1 C water until smooth. Add 2 Tbl sugar and 1/2 C sifted flour. Stir until smooth. Cover and set aside.

Melt 1 LB butter, set aside to cool.

Scald 1 C milk, set aside to cool.

Beat 12 jumbo eggs until frothy. Add 3 1/4 C sugar and melted butter, cream well. Add 2 tsp vanilla and 1 tsp salt. Add milk. Add yeast mixture. Mix well.

Drain raisins and add them.

Add 15 C sifted flour, a cup at a time. Knead dough 7 minutes, adding flour as needed.

Lightly butter a large Tupperware bowl. Put 1/2 of dough in, spread out and turn over. Cover. Repeat with 2nd half of dough in another container. Place in warm oven. Punch down after 2 1/2 - 3 hours. Let rise again 1 more hour. With lightly floured hands push down dough one last time and turn over.

Weigh into 12 oz balls. Divide each ball into 3 parts. On lightly floured surface, braid loaves. Place on parchment paper on large cookie sheet.

Bake at 350 degrees for 10 minutes. Move to lower rack and bake 10 more minutes. Brush with beaten egg yolk. Lower temperature to 325 degrees. Bake 2-3 more minutes depending on brownness. If they are getting too brown on the bottom add a second cookie sheet. Makes 13 loaves.

Lady Fingers

1 LB butter, soft
1 cake yeast
3 eggs, well beaten, put in one cup measure and add milk till full
5 C flour
4 C chopped walnuts mixed with 1 C powdered sugar

Crumble yeast with softened butter. Add eggs/milk mixture and stir. Add flour a little bit at a time. Mix well with hands and form smooth ball. Place in a dish and chill overnight. Make balls approximately a skimpy Tablespoon in size. Roll in powdered sugar. Keep in refrigerator and only take out 6 at a time. Then roll the balls to make an oval. Place in powdered sugar then put nut mixture in center. Roll tightly tucking in ends. Place on ungreased cookie sheet. Put another cookie sheet underneath. Bake at 375 degrees for 15-18 minutes.

Mom's Lady Fingers were always perfect, uniformly matched in size and shape. Mine, not so much. In fact, the first time I attempted to make these alone after my mom passed away I mixed up a double batch. It took quite a long time to roll them out and complete the baking process. They tasted just like mom's! But the next morning I couldn't lift my arm. I found out soon after that I'd had a bone spur that sawed right through my rotator cuff during the rolling motion. I ended up having rotator cuff surgery. Not fun.

Chapter 12:

Pictures

This is the former Whitacre Greer plant where my grandfather worked. It was within walking distance from the house where the family lived. See those smokestacks? They are the very ones my dad climbed in the story on page 19.

This is all that remained of the smokestacks back in 2010. They have since been demolished.

Downtown Waynesburg, Ohio as it looked back when my dad was a young boy. This was the site of the famous sled story featured on pages 11, 13 and 14.

Waynesburg Carriage. This is where the car was kept as described in the story on page 99.

The brickyard houses as they looked back in the day...

This huge silo was part of the big barn described in many of dad's stories. It is featured on page 11. I especially like the barn story on pages 80-81.

This crossroads sign still stands today.

Waynesburg School. So many stories from this building! See Chapter 3: *School Days*.

An old post card depicting the Big Sandy River. This played a big part in many of the stories.

June 18, 1938, Victor DiCola marries Josephine Vitale.

Dad proudly gave away these handmade Nativity mangers. He would take a walk in the woods and gather bark and twigs from dead tree branches then construct each crib to create a log cabin effect. He lined each crib with hay and added a music box that plays "Silent Night". He said: *"I had no drawing (for the crib). I just made it. Everyone loved it. They went crazy for it. They all wanted me to make one for them..."* We treasure these creations and will hand them down to the grandkids and great-grandkids.

The traditional peeling of the orange. See page 131.

The annual burning of the Brazil nut on Christmas Eve. See page 132.

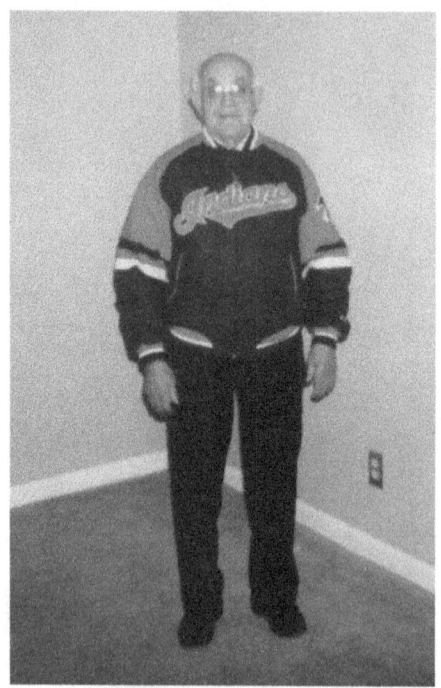

World's greatest Cleveland Indians fan.

Doesn't that look like a halo behind dad's head?

Our favorite night of the year. This was the Last Christmas Eve
(From left) Row 1: Pat, Mom, Dad, Maryanne Row 2: Jim, Fran, Vic, Ceal, Dorothy, Lee, Skip

About the Author

Photo by Julie DiTommaso

Maryanne Shaw has 19 years of marketing and writing experience. She is a successful ad copywriter covering topics from spirituality to natural health. Author of the bestselling memoir, *The 9 Week Miracle.* Her books *Angelwhispers: Listen for them in your life* and *Angel Stories from Across America* were written under the pen name, Marcy D Nicholas. Schedule Maryanne to speak for your group or event. She and her husband, Skip, live in Ohio.

For more information visit **www.maryanneshaw.com**

Valued Customer Reorder Form

Order this...	If you want a book on...	Cost...	Number of Copies...
NEW **Victor's Story** a father teaches his daughter life's most important lessons	True story of Victor's amazing life that spanned 94 years. Filled with Victor's stories and anecdotes from his boyhood days in Waynesburg, Ohio through his adult life including his very special angel stories. The 7 Life Lessons through a daughter's eyes will inspire you to live the life you were meant to lead.	$12.95	
The 9 Week Miracle	True story of a son's survival after being burned 46% of his body in a freak accident. Its message of triumph over adversity leads to the discovery of the 7 Life Lessons we all need to overcome in our own headships. Join Nick *The 9 Week Miracle*. You'll never look at life the same way again.	$9.95	
Angelwhispers: *Listen for them in your life...*	The coincidences that happen in our lives, the little nudges in our minds... that is our angels! Learn to recognize the *Angelwhispers* in your daily life for joy, blessings and abundance.	$9.95	
Angel Stories from Across America	Angel encounters, stories, messages and accounts from readers all across the country. Sure to inspire you with its descriptions of hope and faith in action for everyday including the times of adversity we all face.	$9.95	
Amish Gardening Secrets	You too can learn the special gardening secrets the Amish use to produce huge tomato plants and bountiful harvests. Information packed 800-plus collection for you to tinker with and enjoy.	$9.95	
		Sub total	
	Postage & Handling (1 - 3 books)	$3.98	
	(4 or more books)	$4.98	
		TOTAL	

90-Day Money-Back Guarantee

Please rush me the items marked above. I understand that I must be completely satisfied or I can return any item within 90 days with proof of purchase for a full and prompt refund of my purchase price.

I am enclosing $_____ by: ❑ Check ❑ Money Order
(Make checks payable to Shaw Creative)

Charge my credit card Signature _____

Card No. _____ Exp. Date _____

Name _____

Address _____

City _____ State _____ Zip _____

Telephone Number (_____)_____

❑ Yes! I'd like to know about specials and new books as they become available. My email address is: _____

Mail To: **Shaw Creative** • PO Box 703, • Uniontown, Ohio 44685
http://www.maryanneshaw.com

NEW

VICTOR'S STORY: a father teaches his daughter life's most important lessons

Victor knew that life's priorities should be God first, then family and then career and he lived this example every day. This heartwarming book will move you one minute and have you laughing out loud the next. Truly the story of an amazing life...

THE 9 WEEK MIRACLE

A remarkable journey demonstrating the inherent goodness that exists in people, even perfect strangers. Their willingness to help bridge the gap between suffering and healing was evident in the *Amish garage-raising*. A remarkable event! It is a saga of faith, gritty determination and endurance.

ANGELWHISPERS: *Listen for them in your life...*

Do you Believe in Angels? Angels are ready to help us in lots of ways. They can protect us from danger, reduce our fears, pain, worries and even help us find ways to cope with our problems. Learn the techniques in this book to improve every aspect of your life – *even your wealth!*

ANGEL STORIES FROM ACROSS AMERICA

More words of hope and encouragement from the author of Angelwhispers: Listen for them in your life. This new book has true angel stories of encounters with loved ones from readers from all over the country!

AMISH GARDENING SECRETS

There's something for everyone in *Amish Gardening Secrets*. This BIG collection contains over 800 gardening hints, suggestions, time savers and tonics that have been passed down over the years in Amish communities and elsewhere.

> All these important books carry our NO-RISK GUARANTEE. Enjoy them for three full months. If you are not 100% satisfied simply return the book(s) along with proof of purchase, for a prompt, "no questions asked" refund!

http://www.maryanneshaw.com

www.ingramcontent.com/pod-product-compliance
Lightning Source LLC
Chambersburg PA
CBHW060155050426
42446CB00013B/2839